Fixed point theorems with applications to economics and game theory

Fixed point theorems with applications to economics and game theory

KIM C. BORDER

California Institute of Technology

CAMBRIDGE
UNIVERSITY PRESS

PUBLISHED BY THE PRESS SYNDICATE OF THE UNIVERSITY OF CAMBRIDGE
The Pitt Building, Trumpington Street, Cambridge, United Kingdom

CAMBRIDGE UNIVERSITY PRESS
The Edinburgh Building, Cambridge CB2 2RU, UK http://www.cup.cam.ac.uk
40 West 20th Street, New York, NY 10011-4211, USA http://www.cup.org
10 Stamford Road, Oakleigh, Melbourne 3166, Australia

First published 1985
Reprinted 1999

A catalogue record for this book is available from the British Library

Library of Congress Cataloguing-in-Publication data
Border, Kim C.
Fixed point theorems with applications to economics
and game theory.
Includes bibliographical references and index.
1. Fixed point theory. 2. Economics, Mathematical.
3. Game theory. I. Title.
QA329.9.B67 1985 515.7'248 84-19925

ISBN 0 521 26564 9 hardback
ISBN 0 521 38808 2 paperback

Transferred to digital printing 2003

Contents

Preface

Fixed point theorems are the basic mathematical tools used in showing the existence of solution concepts in game theory and economics. While there are many excellent texts available on fixed point theory, most of them are inaccessible to a typical well-trained economist. These notes are intended to be a nonintimidating introduction to the subject of fixed point theory with particular emphasis on economic applications. While I have tried to integrate the mathematics and applications, these notes are not a comprehensive introduction to either general equilibrium theory or game theory. There are already a number of excellent texts in these areas. Debreu [1959] and Luce and Raiffa [1957] are classics. More recent texts include Hildenbrand and Kirman [1976], Ichiishi [1983], Moulin [1982] and Owen [1982]. Instead I have tried to cover material that gets left out of these texts, and to present it in such a way as to make it quickly and easily accessible to people who want to apply fixed point theorems, not refine them. I have made an effort to present useful theorems fairly early on in the text. This leads to a certain amount of compromise. In order to keep prerequisites to a minimum, the theorems are not generally stated in their most general form and the proofs presented are not necessarily the most elegant. I have tried to keep the level of mathematical sophistication on a par with, say, Rudin [1976]. In particular, only finite-dimensional spaces are used. While many of the theorems presented here are true in arbitrary locally convex spaces, no attempt has been made to cover the infinite-dimensional results. I have however deliberately tried to present proofs that generalize easily to infinite dimensional spaces whenever possible.

In an effort to show interconnections between the various results I have often given more than one proof. In fact, Chapters 9 and 21 consist largely of such interconnections. A good way to treat these chapters is as a collection of exercises with very elaborate hints. I have also tried as far as possible to indicate the sources and history of the various theorems. I apologize in advance for any omissions of credit or priority.

In preparing these notes I have had the benefit of the comments of my students and colleagues. I would particularly like to thank Don Brown, Tatsuro Ichiishi, Scott Johnson, Jim Jordan, Richard McKelvey, Wayne Shafer, Jim Snyder, and especially Ed Green.

I would also like to thank Linda Benjamin, Edith Huang and Carl Lydick for all their help in the physical preparation of this manuscript.

For the third printing, a number of errors have been corrected. I thank H. C. Petith, John Ledyard, Ed Green, Richard Boylan, Patrick Legros, Mark Olson, Guofu Tan, and Dongping Yin for pointing out many of them.

CHAPTER 1

Introduction: Models and mathematics

1.1 Mathematical Models of Economies and Games

Supply and demand: These are the determinants of prices in a market economy. Prices are determined by markets so that the supply of commodities from producers is equal to the demand for commodities by consumers. Such a state of equality is known as a market equilibrium. In a large market economy the number of prices determined is enormous. Aside from the practical difficulty of computing and communicating all those prices, how can we even be sure that it is possible to find prices that will equate supply and demand in all markets at once? Mathematicians will recognize the problem as one of proving the existence of a solution to a set of (nonlinear) equations. The first successful efforts by mathematicians toward answering this question took place in the 1930's, in a workshop conducted by Karl Menger in Vienna. The seminars were attended by many of the finest mathematicians of the period and produced the pathbreaking papers of Wald [1935; 1936]. Also published in the proceedings of Menger's seminar was an important piece by von Neumann [1937]. At about the same time, mathematicians began an intensive study of games and what outcomes ought to be expected from a game played by rational players. Most of the proposed outcomes are characterized as some form of "equilibrium." That is, the outcome of a game ought to be a situation where no player (or perhaps no group of players) wants to change his play. Again the question arises as to if and when such a combination of plays exist. The notion of mixed strategy had been developed by Borel [1921], but the first major result in the field, the minimax theorem, is due to von Neumann [1928]. It turns out that the same mathematical tools are useful in value theory and game theory, at least for proving the existence of equilibrium. This monograph is not intended to be an introduction to either value theory or game theory, but rather an introduction to the mathematical tools of fixed point theorems and their applications to value theory and game theory.

This first chapter is an outline of the various formal models of games and economies that have been developed in order to rigorously and formally analyze the sorts of questions described above. The purpose of this brief introduction is to show how the purely mathematical results presented in the following chapters are relevant to the economic and game theoretic problems.

The approach to modeling economies used here is generally referred to as the Arrow-Debreu model. The presentation of this model will be quite brief. A more detailed description and justification of the model can be found in Koopmans [1957] or Debreu [1959].

The fundamental idealization made in modeling an economy is the notion of a commodity. We suppose that it is possible to classify all the different goods and services in the world into a finite number, m, of commodities, which are available in infinitely divisible units. The *commodity space* is then $\mathbf{R}^m$. A vector in $\mathbf{R}^m$ specifies a list of quantities of each commodity. It is commodity vectors that are exchanged, manufactured and consumed in the course of economic activity, not individual commodities; although a typical exchange involves a zero quantity of most commodities. A price vector lists the value of a unit of each commodity and so belongs to $\mathbf{R}^m$. Thus the value of commodity vector x at prices p is $\sum_{i=1}^{m} p_i x_i = p \cdot x$.

While some physical goods are clearly indivisible, we are frequently interested not in the physical goods, but in the services they provide, which, if we measure the flow of services in units of time, we can take to be measured in infinitely divisible units. Both the assumptions of infinite divisibility and the existence of only a finite number of distinct commodities can be dispensed with, and economists are not limited to analyzing economies where these assumptions hold. To consider economies with an infinite number of distinct and possibly indivisible commodities requires the use of more sophisticated and subtle mathematics than is presented here. In this case the commodity space is an infinite-dimensional vector space and the price vector belongs to the dual space of the commodity space. Some fine examples of analyses using an infinite-dimensional commodity space are Mas-Colell [1975], Bewley [1972], or Aliprantis and Brown [1983], to name a few.

The principal participants in an economy are the consumers. The ultimate purpose of the economic organization is to provide commodity vectors for final consumption by consumers. We will assume that there is a given finite number of consumers. Not every commodity vector is admissible as a final consumption for a consumer. The set $X_i \subset \mathbf{R}^m$ of all admissible consumption vectors for consumer i is his *consumption set*. There are a variety of restrictions that might be embodied in the consumption set. One possible restriction that might be placed on admissible consumption vectors is that they be nonnegative. An alternative restriction is that the consumption set be bounded below. Under this interpretation, negative quantities of a commodity in a final consumption vector mean that the consumer is supplying the commodity as a service. The lower bound puts a limit in the services that a consumer can provide. The lower bound could also be a minimum requirement of some commodity for the consumer. In a private ownership economy consumers are also partially characterized by their initial *endowment* of commodities. This is represented as a point w_i in the commodity space. These are the resources the consumer owns.

In a market economy a consumer must purchase his consumption vector at the market prices. The set of admissible commodity vectors that he can afford at prices p given an income M_i is called his *budget set* and is just $\{x \in X_i : p \cdot x \leqslant M_i\}$. The budget set might well be empty. The problem faced by a consumer in a market economy is to choose a consumption vector or set of them from the budget set. To do this, the consumer must have some criterion for choosing. One way to formalize the criterion is to assume that the consumer has a utility index, that is, a real-valued function u_i defined on the set of consumption vectors. The idea is that a consumer would prefer to consume vector x rather than vector y if $u_i(x) > u_i(y)$ and would be indifferent if $u_i(x) = u_i(y)$. The solution to the consumer's problem is then to find all the vectors x which maximize u on the budget set. Does even this simple problem have a solution?: Not necessarily. It could be that for any x there is a y in the budget set with $u_i(y) > u_i(x)$. If some restrictions are placed on the utility index, namely requiring it to be continuous, and on the budget set, requiring it to be compact, then it follows from a well-known theorem of Weierstrass that there are vectors that maximize the value of u_i over the budget set.

These assumptions on the consumer's criterion are somewhat severe, for they force the consumer's preferences to mirror the order properties of the real numbers. In particular; if $u_i(x^1) = u_i(x^2)$ and $u_i(x^2) = u_i(x^3),\ldots,u_i(x^{k-1}) = u(x^k)$, then $u(x^1) = u(x^k)$. One can easily imagine situations where a consumer is indifferent between vectors x^1 and x^2, and between x^2 and x^3, etc., but not between x^1 and x^k. The compounding of slight differences between commodity vectors can lead to a significant difference between x^1 and x^k. Fortunately, these sorts of problems do not preclude the existence of a solution to the consumer's problem. There are weaker assumptions we can make about preferences that still guarantee the existence of "best" consumption vectors in the budget set. Two approaches are discussed in Chapter 7 below. Both approaches involve the use of binary relations or correspondences to describe a consumer's preferences. This is done by letting $U_i(x)$ denote the set of all consumption vectors which consumer i strictly prefers to x. In terms of the utility index, $U_i(x) = \{y : u_i(y) > u_i(x)\}$. If we take the relations U_i as the primitive way of describing preferences, then we are not bound to assume transitivity. The assumptions that we make on preferences in Chapter 7 include a weak continuity assumption. One approach assumes that there are no cycles in the strict preference relation, the other approach assumes a weak form of convexity of the preferred sets. The set of solutions to a consumer's problem for given prices is his *demand set.*

The suppliers' problem is conceptually simpler: Suppliers are motivated by profits. Each supplier j has a *production set* Y_j of technologically feasible supply vectors. A supply vector specifies the quantities of each commodity supplied and the amount of each commodity used as an input. Inputs are denoted by negative quantities and outputs by positive ones. The profit or net income associated with supply vector y at prices p is just $\sum_{i=1}^{m} p_i y_i = p \cdot y$. The supplier's problem is then to choose a y from the set of technologically feasible supply vectors which maximizes the associated profit. As in the consumer's problem, there may be no solution, as it may pay to increase the outputs and inputs indefinitely at ever increasing profits. The set of profit maximizing production vectors is the *supply set.*

Thus, given a price vector p, there is a set of supply vectors y_j for each supplier, determined by maximizing profits; and a set of demand vectors x_i for each consumer, determined by preference maximization. In a private ownership economy the consumers' incomes are determined by the prices through the wages received for services supplied, through the sale of resources they own and from the dividends paid by firms out of profits. Let α_j^i denote consumer i's share of the profits of firm j. The budget set for consumer i given prices p is then

$$\{x \in X_i : p \cdot x \leqslant p \cdot w_i + \sum_j \alpha_j^i p \cdot y_j\}$$

The set of sums of demand vectors minus sums of supply vectors is the *excess demand set*, $E(p)$. The equilibrium notion that we will use was formalized by Walras [1874]. A price vector p is a *Walrasian equilibrium price* vector if some combination of these supply and demand vectors adds up to zero, i.e., $0 \in E(p)$. Alternately, some commodities might be allowed to be in excess supply at equilibrium, provided their price is zero. Such a situation is called a *(Walrasian) free disposal equilibrium.* The price p is a free disposal equilibrium price if there is some $z \in E(p)$ satisfying $z \leqslant 0$ and whenever $z_i < 0$, then $p_i = 0$. The question of when an equilibrium exists is addressed in Chapters 8, 18 and 20 below. Of fundamental importance to the approach taken in sections 8 and 18 is a property of excess demands known as Walras' law. Informally, Walras' law says that if the profits of all suppliers are returned to consumers as dividends, then the value at prices p of any excess demand vector must be nonpositive. This is because the value of each consumer's demand must be no more than his income and the sum of all incomes must be the sum of all profits from suppliers. Thus the value of total supply must be at least as large as the value of total demand. If each consumer spends all his income, then these two values are equal and the value of excess demand must be zero.

A *game* is any situation where a number of players must each make a choice of an action (strategy) and then, based on all these choices, some consequence occurs. When certain aspects of the game are random as in, say, poker, then it is convenient to treat nature as a player. Nature then chooses the random action to be taken. A player's strategy itself might involve a random variable. Such a strategy is called a *mixed strategy.* For instance, if there are a finite number n of "pure" strategies, then we can identify a mixed strategy with a vector in $\mathbf{R}^n$, the components of which indicate the probability of taking the corresponding "pure" action. (In these notes we will restrict our attention to the case where the set of strategies can be identified with a subset of a euclidean space.) A strategy vector consists of a list of the choices of strategy for each player. Each strategy vector completely determines the outcome of the game. (Although the outcome may be a random variable, its distribution is determined by the strategy vector.) Each player has preferences over the outcomes which may be represented by a utility index, or his preferences may only have the weaker properties used in the analysis of consumer demand. The preferences over outcomes induce preferences over strategy vectors, so we can start out by assuming that the player's preferences are defined over strategy vectors. A *game in strategic form* is specified by a list of strategy spaces and preferences over strategy vectors for each player.

When playing the game noncooperatively, a *(Nash) equilibrium* strategy vector is one in which no player, acting alone, can benefit from changing his strategy choice. The existence of noncooperative equilibria is discussed in Chapter 19 below. A variation on the notion of a noncooperative game is that of an *abstract economy.* In an abstract economy, the set of strategies available to a player depends on the strategy choices of the other players. Take, for example, the problem of finding an equilibrium price vector for a market economy. This can be converted into a game-like framework where the strategy sets of consumers are their consumption sets demands and those of suppliers are their production sets. To incorporate the budget constraints of the consumers we must introduce another player, often called the auctioneer, whose set of strategies consists of price vectors. The set of available strategies for a consumer, i.e., his budget set, thus depends on the auctioneer's strategy choice through the price, and the suppliers' strategy choices through dividends. The equilibrium of an abstract economy is also discussed in Chapter 19.

A strategy vector is a Nash equilibrium if no individual player can gain by changing his strategy, given that no one else does. If players can coordinate their strategies, then this notion of equilibrium is less appealing. The cooperative theory of games attempts to take into account the power of *coalitions* of players. The cooperative analysis of games tends to use different tools from the noncooperative analysis. The fundamental way of describing a game is by means of a *characteristic function.* The role of strategies is pushed into the background in this analysis. Instead, the characteristic function describes for each coalition of players the set of outcomes that the coalition can guarantee for its members. The outcomes may be expressed either in terms of utility or in terms of physical outcomes. The term "guarantee" can be taken as primitive or it can be derived in various ways from a strategic form game. The α-characteristic function associated with a strategic form game assumes that coalition B can guarantee outcome x if it has a strategy which yields x regardless of which strategy the complementary coalition plays. The β-characteristic function assumes that coalition B can guarantee x if for each choice of strategy by the complementary coalition, B can choose a strategy (possibly depending on the complement's choice) which yields at least x. These two notions were explicitly formalized by Aumann and Peleg [1960].

In order for an outcome to be a cooperative equilibrium, it cannot be profitable for a coalition to overturn the outcome. A coalition can *block* or *improve upon* an outcome x if there is some outcome y which it can guarantee for its members and which they all prefer to x. The *core* of a characteristic function game is the set of all unblocked outcomes. The same idea motivates the definition of a *strong (Nash) equilibrium* in a strategic form game. A strong equilibrium is a strategy vector with the property that no coalition can jointly change its strategy in such a way as to make all of its members better off.

Theorems giving sufficient conditions for the existence of strong equilibria and nonempty cores are presented in Chapter 23.

1.2 Recurring Mathematical Themes

These notes are about fixed point theorems. Let f be a function mapping a set K into itself. A *fixed point* of f is a point $z \in K$ satisfying $f(z) = z$. The basic theorem on fixed points which we will use is the Brouwer fixed point theorem (6.6), which asserts that if K is a compact convex subset of euclidean space, then every continuous function mapping K into itself has a fixed point. There are several ways to prove this theorem. The approach taken in these notes is via Sperner's lemma (4.1). Sperner's lemma is a combinatorial result about labeled simplicial subdivisions. The reason this approach to the proof of the theorem is taken is that Sperner's lemma provides insight into computational algorithms for finding approximations to fixed points. We can formulate precisely the notion that completely labeled simplexes are approximations of fixed points (10.5).

A problem closely related to finding fixed points of a function is that of finding zeroes of a function. For if z is a fixed point of f, then z is a zero of $(Id - f)$, where Id denotes the identity function. Likewise if z is a zero of g, then z is a fixed point of $(Id - g)$. Thus fixed point theorems can be useful in showing the existence of a solution to a vector-valued equation.

What is not necessarily so clear is that fixed point theory is useful in showing the existence of solutions to sets of simultaneous inequalities. It is frequently easy to show the existence of solutions to a single inequality. What is needed then is to show that the intersection of the solutions for all the inequalities is nonempty. The Knaster-Kuratowski-Mazurkiewicz lemma (5.4) provides a set of sufficient conditions on a family of sets that guarantees that its intersection is nonempty. It turns out that the K-K-M lemma can also be easily proved from Sperner's lemma and that we can approximate the intersection of the family of sets by completely labeled subsimplexes (Theorem 10.2). The K-K-M lemma also allows one to deduce the Brouwer fixed point theorem and vice versa (9.1 and 9.3).

A particular application of finding the intersection of a family of sets is that of finding maximal elements of a binary relation. A *binary relation* U on a set K is a subset of $K \times K$ or alternatively a *correspondence* mapping K into itself. We can write yUx or $y \in U(x)$ to mean that y stands in the relation U to x. A *maximal element* of the binary relation U is a point x such that no point y satisfies yUx, i.e., $U(x) = \varnothing$. Thus the set of maximal elements of U is equal to

$$\bigcap_y \{x : yUx\}^c.$$

Theorem 7.2 provides sufficient conditions for a binary relation to have maximal elements. Theorem 7.2 can be used to prove the fixed point theorem (9.8) and many other useful results (e.g., 8.1, 8.6, 8.8, 17.1, 18.1). Not surprisingly, the Brouwer theorem can be used to prove Theorem 7.2 (9.12).

The fixed point theorem can be generalized from functions carrying a set into itself to correspondences carrying points of a set to subsets of the set. For a correspondence γ taking K to its power set, we say that $z \in K$ is a *fixed point* of γ if $z \in \gamma(z)$. Appropriate notions of continuity for correspondences are discussed in Chapter 11. One analogue of the Brouwer theorem for correspondences is the Kakutani fixed point theorem (15.3). The basic technique used in extending results for continuous functions to results for correspondences with closed graph is to approximate the correspondence by means of a continuous function (Lemma 13.3). Another useful technique that can sometimes be used in dealing with correspondences is to find a continuous function lying inside the graph of the correspondence. The selection theorems 14.3 and 14.7 provide conditions under which this can be done. The tool used to construct the continuous functions used in approximation or selection theorems is the partition of unity (2.19).

All the arguments involving partitions of unity used in these notes have a common form, which is sketched here, and used in many guises below. For each $x \in K$, there is a property $P(x)$, and it is desired to find a continuous function g such that $g(x)$ has property $P(x)$ for each x. Suppose that for each x, $\{y : y \text{ has property } P(x)\}$ is convex and for each y, $\{x : y \text{ has property } P(x)\}$ is open. For each x, let $y(x)$ have property $P(x)$. In general $y(\cdot)$ is not continuous. However, take a partition of unity $\{f_x\}$ subordinate to $\{\{z : y(x) \text{ has property } P(z)\} : x \in K\}$ and set $g(z) = \sum_x f_x(z)y(x)$.

Since $f_x(z) > 0$ only if $y(x)$ has property $P(z)$, it follows from the convexity of $\{y : y \text{ has property } P(z)\}$ that $g(z)$ satisfies $P(z)$. Sometimes the above argument is turned on its head to prove that there is an x for which nothing has property $P(x)$. That is, it may be known (or can easily be shown) that no continuous function g as above can exist, and thus there must be some x for which nothing satisfies property $P(x)$. We can view the property $P(x)$ as a correspondence $x \mapsto\!\!\!\to \{y : y \text{ has property } P(x)\}$. Thus the role of partitions of unity in selection theorems is immediate. Further, if we have a binary relation U and say that y satisfies $P(x)$ if yUx, then it is a virtual metatheorem that every argument involving maximal elements of binary relations has an analogue using partitions of unity and vice versa. This theme occurs repeatedly in the proofs presented below.

CHAPTER 2

Convexity

2.0 Basic Notation

Denote the reals by $\mathbf{R}$, the nonnegative reals by $\mathbf{R}_+$ and the strictly positive reals by $\mathbf{R}_{++}$. The m-dimensional euclidean space is denoted $\mathbf{R}^m$. The unit coordinate vectors in $\mathbf{R}^m$ are denoted by $e^1,...,e^m$. When referring to a space of dimension $m+1$, the coordinates may be numbered $0,...,m$. Thus $e^0,...,e^m$ are the unit coordinate vectors in $\mathbf{R}^{m+1}$. When referring to vectors, subscripts will generally denote components and superscripts will be used to distinguish different vectors.

Define the following partial orders on $\mathbf{R}^m$. Say that $x > y$ or $y < x$ if $x_i > y_i$ for $i = 1,...,m$; and $x \geqslant y$ or $y \leqslant x$ if $x_i \geqslant y_i$ for $i = 1,...,m$. Thus $\mathbf{R}^m_+ = \{x \in \mathbf{R}^m : x \geqslant 0\}$ and $\mathbf{R}^m_{++} = \{x \in \mathbf{R}^m : x > 0\}$.

The inner product of two vectors in $\mathbf{R}^m$ is given by $p \cdot x = \sum_{i=1}^{m} p_i x_i$. The euclidean norm is $|x| = (\sum_{i=1}^{m} x_i^2)^{1/2} = (p \cdot p)^{1/2}$. The ball of radius ε centered at x, $\{y \in \mathbf{R}^m : |x - y| < \varepsilon\}$ is denoted $B_\varepsilon(x)$. For $E \subset \mathbf{R}^m$, let *cl* E or $\bar{E}$ denote its closure and *int* E denote its interior. Also let *dist* $(x,F) = \inf\{|x - y| : y \in F\}$, and $N_\varepsilon(F) = \bigcup_{x \in F} B_\varepsilon(x)$.

If E and F are subsets of $\mathbf{R}^m$, define $E + F = \{x + y : x \in E; y \in F\}$ and $\lambda F = \{\lambda x : x \in F\}$.

For a set E, $|E|$ denotes the cardinality of E.

2.1 Definition

A set $C \subset \mathbf{R}^m$ is *convex* if for every $x,y \in C$ and $\lambda \in [0,1]$, $\lambda x + (1 - \lambda)y \in C$. For vectors $x^1,...,x^n$ and nonnegative scalars $\lambda_1, \ldots, \lambda_n$ satisfying $\sum_{i=1}^{n} \lambda_i = 1$, the vector $\sum_{i=1}^{n} \lambda_i x^i$ is called a *(finite) convex combination* of $x^1, \ldots, x^n$. A *strictly positive convex combination* is a convex combination where each scalar $\lambda_i > 0$.

2.2 Definition
For $A \subset \mathbf{R}^m$, the *convex hull* of A, denoted *co* A, is the set of all finite convex combinations from A, i.e., *co* A is the set of all vectors x of the form

$$x = \sum_{i=1}^{n} \lambda_i x^i$$

for some n, where each $x^i \in A$, $\lambda_1, \ldots, \lambda_n \in \mathbf{R}_+$ and $\sum_{i=1}^{n} \lambda_i = 1$.

2.3 Caratheodory's Theorem
Let $E \subset \mathbf{R}^m$. If $x \in co\ E$, then x can be written as a convex combination of no more than $m+1$ points in E, i.e., there are $z^0,\ldots,z^m \in E$ and $\lambda_0, \ldots, \lambda_m \in \mathbf{R}_+$ with $\sum_{i=0}^{m} \lambda_i = 1$ such that

$$x = \sum_{i=0}^{m} \lambda_i z^i.$$

2.4 Proof
Exercise. Hint: For $z \in \mathbf{R}^m$ set $\tilde{z} = (1, z_1, \ldots, z_m) \in \mathbf{R}^{m+1}$. The problem then reduces to showing that if $\tilde{x}$ is a nonnegative linear combination of $\tilde{z}^1, \ldots, \tilde{z}^k$, then it is a nonnegative linear combination at most $m+1$ of the $\tilde{z}$'s. Use induction on k.

2.5 Exercise
(a) If for all i in some index set I, C_i is convex, then $\bigcap_{i \in I} C_i$ and $\prod_{i \in I} C_i$ are convex.
(b) If C_1 and C_2 are convex, then so are $C_1 + C_2$ and λC_1.
(c) $co\ A = \bigcap \{C : A \subset C;\ C \text{ is } convex\}$.
(d) If A is open, then *co* A is open.
(e) If K is compact, then *co* K is compact. (Hint: Use 2.3.)
(f) If A is convex, then *int* A and *cl* A are convex.

2.6 Example
The convex hull of F may fail to be closed if F is not compact, even if F is closed. For instance, set

$$F = \{(x_1, x_2) \in \mathbf{R}^2 : x_2 \geqslant |1/x_1| \text{ and } |x_1| \geqslant 1\}.$$

Then F is closed, but $co\ F = \{(x_1, x_2) \in \mathbf{R}^2 : x_2 > 0\}$ is not closed. See Figure 2(a).

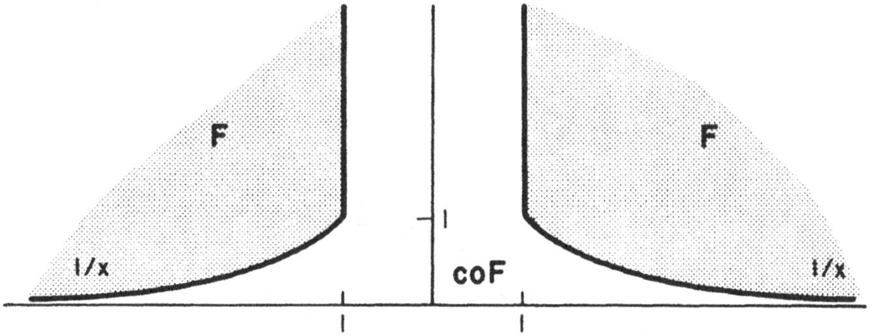

Figure 2(a)

2.7 Exercise

Let $E,F \subset \mathbf{R}^m$. For $x \in E$, let $g(x) = dist\ (x,F)$, then $g : E \to \mathbf{R}_+$ is continuous. If F is closed, then there exists $y \in F$ satisfying $g(x) = |x - y|$. If F is convex as well, then such a y is unique. In this case the function $h : E \to F$ defined by $|x - h(x)| = g(x)$ is continuous. (For $x \in E \cap F$, h is the identity.)

2.8 Definition

A *hyperplane* in $\mathbf{R}^m$ is a set of the form $\{x \in \mathbf{R}^m : p \cdot x = c\}$ where $0 \neq p \in \mathbf{R}^m$ and $c \in \mathbf{R}$. A set of the form $\{x : p \cdot x \leqslant c\}$ (resp. $\{x : p \cdot x < c\}$) is called a *closed* (resp. *open*) *half space*. Two sets A and B are said to be *strictly separated* by a hyperplane if there is some nonzero $p \in \mathbf{R}^m$ and some $c \in \mathbf{R}$ such that for each $x \in A$ and $y \in B$

$$p \cdot x < c < p \cdot y.$$

That is, A and B are in distinct open half spaces. (We will sometimes write this as $p \cdot A < c < p \cdot B$.)

2.9 Theorem (Separating Hyperplane Theorem)

Let C and K be disjoint nonempty convex subsets of $\mathbf{R}^m$ and let C be closed and K be compact. Then C and K can be strictly separated by a hyperplane.

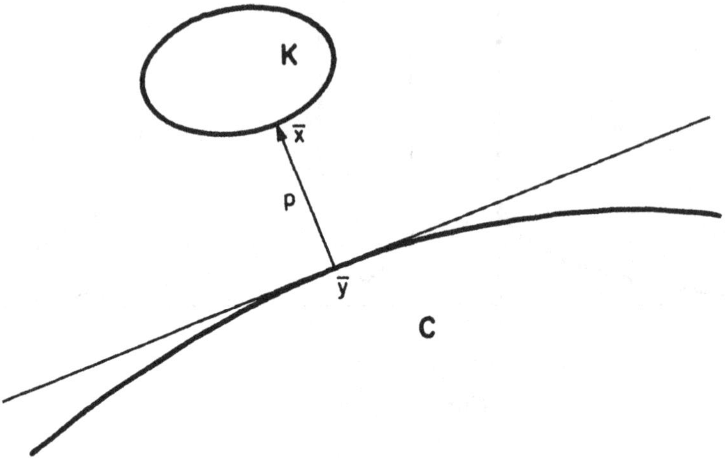

Figure 2(b)

2.10 Proof

Exercise. Hint: Put $f(x) = dist\ (x,C)$; then f is continuous and attains its minimum on K, say at $\bar{x}$. Let $\bar{y}$ be the unique point in C (2.7) such that $f(\bar{x}) = |\bar{x} - \bar{y}|$. Put $p = \bar{x} - \bar{y}$. See Figure 2(b). Then $0 < |p|^2 = p \cdot p = p \cdot (\bar{x} - \bar{y})$, so $p \cdot \bar{x} > p \cdot \bar{y}$. What needs to be shown is that $p \cdot \bar{y} \geqslant p \cdot y$ for all $y \in C$ and $p \cdot \bar{x} \leqslant p \cdot x$ for all $x \in K$:

Let $y \in C$ and put $y^\lambda = (1 - \lambda)\bar{y} + \lambda y \in C$. Then

$$\begin{aligned}|\bar{x} - y^\lambda|^2 &= [\lambda(\bar{x} - y) + (1 - \lambda)(\bar{x} - \bar{y})] \\ &\quad \cdot [\lambda(\bar{x} - y) + (1 - \lambda)(\bar{x} - \bar{y})] \\ &= (1 - \lambda)^2|\bar{x} - \bar{y}|^2 + 2\lambda(1 - \lambda)[(\bar{x} - \bar{y}) \cdot (\bar{x} - y)] \\ &\quad + \lambda^2|\bar{x} - y|^2.\end{aligned}$$

Differentiating with respect to λ and evaluating at $\lambda = 0$ yields

$$\begin{aligned}-2(\bar{x} - \bar{y})^2 + 2(\bar{x} - \bar{y}) \cdot (\bar{x} - y) &= -2p \cdot (\bar{x} - \bar{y} - \bar{x} + y) \\ &= -2p \cdot (y - \bar{y}).\end{aligned}$$

Since $\bar{y}$ minimizes $|\bar{x} - y|^2$ on C, this derivative must be $\geqslant 0$. Thus $p \cdot \bar{y} \geqslant p \cdot y$.

A similar argument for $x \in K$ completes the proof.

2.11 Definition

A *cone* is a nonempty subset of $\mathbf{R}^m$ closed under multiplication by nonnegative scalars. That is, C is a cone if whenever $x \in C$ and $\lambda \in \mathbf{R}_+$, then $\lambda x \in C$.

2.12 Exercise

(a) The intersection of cones is a cone.

(b) If C is a cone, then $0 \in C$.

(c) Any set $E \subset \mathbf{R}^m$ generates a cone, $\{\lambda x : x \in E, \lambda \in \mathbf{R}_+\}$. The cone generated by E is the intersection of all cones containing E.

(d) A cone is convex if and only if it is closed under addition, i.e., a cone C is convex if and only if $x,y \in C$ implies $x + y \in C$.

2.13 Definition

If $C \subset \mathbf{R}^m$, the *dual cone* of C, denoted C^*, is

$$\{p \in \mathbf{R}^m : \forall x \in C \;\; p \cdot x \leqslant 0\}.$$

(*Warning*: The definition of dual cone varies among authors. Frequently the inequality in the definition is reversed and the dual cone is defined to be $\{p : \forall x \in C \;\; p \cdot x \geqslant 0\}$. This latter definition is standard with mathematicians, but not universal. The definition used here follows Debreu [1959] and Gale [1960], two standard references in mathematical economics. The other definition may be found, for example, in Nikaido [1968] or Gaddum [1952].)

2.14 Exercise

(a) If C is a cone, then C^* is a closed convex cone and $(C^*)^* = cl\,(co\; C)$.

(b) $(\mathbf{R}^m_+)^* = \{x \in \mathbf{R}^m : x \leqslant 0\}$.

(c) If C is a cone and lies in the open half space $\{x : p \cdot x < c\}$, then it must be that $c > 0$ and C in fact lies in the half space $\{x : p \cdot x \leqslant 0\}$.

2.15 Proposition

Let $C \subset \mathbf{R}^m$ be a closed convex cone and let $K \subset \mathbf{R}^m$ be compact and convex. Then $K \cap C^* \neq \varnothing$ if and only if

$$\forall p \in C \;\; \exists z \in K \;\; p \cdot z \leqslant 0. \qquad 2.16$$

2.17 Proof

Suppose $K \cap C^* = \varnothing$. Then by 2.9 we can strictly separate K and C^* with a hyperplane. That is, there exists some $q \in \mathbf{R}^m$ such that

$$q \cdot C^* < c < q \cdot K.$$

Since C^* is a cone, we have by 2.14(c) that $c > 0$ and $q \cdot C^* \leqslant 0$. Thus $q \in C^{**} = C$ and $q \cdot K > 0$, contradicting 2.16.

Conversely, let $z \in K \cap C^*$. Then by 2.14(a), $p \cdot z \leqslant 0$ for all $p \in C$, so 2.16 holds.

2.18 Proposition (Gaddum [1952])
Let $C \subset \mathbf{R}^m$ be a closed convex cone. Then C is a linear subspace of $\mathbf{R}^m$ if and only if

$$C^* \cap -C = \{0\}.$$

2.19 Proof (Gaddum [1952])
Let $p \in C^*$, i.e., $p \cdot x \leqslant 0$ for all $x \in C$. Let $p \in C^* \cap -C$. If C is a subspace, then $-C = C$, so $p \in C$ and, substituting p for x, we get $p \cdot p \leqslant 0$, which implies $p = 0$.

If C is not a linear subspace, then there is some $x \in C$ with $x \notin -C$. Following the argument in 2.10, let $\bar{y} \in -C$ minimize the distance to x, and put $p = \bar{y} + (-x)$. Note that $p \neq 0$. Then $p \in -C$, as $-C$ is closed under addition by 2.12(d). By the same argument as in 2.10,

$$p \cdot y \geqslant p \cdot \bar{y} \text{ for all } y \in -C,$$

or

$$p \cdot y \leqslant p \cdot (-\bar{y}) \text{ for all } y \in C.$$

By 2.14(d), it follows that $p \cdot y \leqslant 0$ for all $y \in C$, i.e., $p \in C^*$. Thus $0 \neq p \in C^* \cap -C$.

2.20 Definition
The collection $\{U_\alpha\}$ is an *open cover* of K if each U_α is open and $\bigcup_\alpha U_\alpha \supset K$. A *partition of unity subordinate to* $\{U_\alpha\}$ is a finite set of continuous functions $f_1, \ldots, f_k : K \to \mathbf{R}_+$ such that $\sum_{i=1}^{k} f_i \equiv 1$, and for each i there is some U_{α_i} such that f_i vanishes off U_{α_i}. A collection of functions $\{f_\alpha : E \to \mathbf{R}_+\}$ is a *locally finite partition of unity* if each point has a neighborhood on which all but finitely many f_α vanish, and $\sum_\alpha f_\alpha \equiv 1$.

2.21 Theorem
Let $K \subset \mathbf{R}^m$ be compact and let $\{U_\alpha\}$ be an open cover of K. Then there exists a partition of unity subordinate to $\{U_\alpha\}$.

2.22 Proof
Since K is compact, $\{U_\alpha\}$ has a finite subcover $U_1, \ldots, U_k$. Define $g_i : K \to \mathbf{R}_+$ by $g_i(x) = min\ \{|x - z| : z \in U_i^c\}$. Such a g_i is continuous (2.7) and vanishes off U_i. Furthermore, not all g_i vanish simultaneously as the U_i's are a cover of K. Set $f_i = g_i / \sum_j g_j$. Then $\{f_i, \ldots, f_k\}$ is the desired partition of unity.

2.23 Corollary
If $\{U_1, \ldots, U_k\}$ is a finite open cover of K, then there is a partition of unity $f_1, \ldots, f_k$ such that each f_i vanishes off U_i.

2.24 Remark
A set E is called *paracompact* if it has the property that whenever $\{U_\alpha\}$ is an open cover of E, then there is a locally finite partition of unity subordinated to it. Theorem 2.21 asserts that every compact subset of a euclidean space is paracompact. More is true: Every subset of a euclidean space is paracompact. In fact, every metric space is paracompact. A proof of the following theorem may be found in Willard [1970, 20.9 and 20C].

2.25 Theorem
Let $E \subset \mathbf{R}^m$ and let $\{U_\alpha\}$ be an open cover of E. Then there is a locally finite partition of unity subordinate to $\{U_\alpha\}$.

2.26 Definition
Let $E \subset \mathbf{R}^m$ be convex and let $f : E \to \mathbf{R}$. We say that f is *quasi-concave* if for each $\alpha \in \mathbf{R}$, $\{x \in E : f(x) \geqslant \alpha\}$ is convex; and that f is *quasi-convex* if for each $\alpha \in \mathbf{R}$, $\{x \in E : f(x) \leqslant \alpha\}$ is convex. The function f is quasi-concave if and only if $-f$ is quasi-convex.

2.27 Definition
Let $E \subset \mathbf{R}^m$ and let $f : E \to \mathbf{R}$. We say that f is *upper semi-continuous* on E if for each $\alpha \in \mathbf{R}$, $\{x \in E : f(x) \geqslant \alpha\}$ is closed in E. This of course implies that $\{x \in E : f(x) < \alpha\}$ is open in E. We say that f is *lower semi-continuous* on E if $-f$ is upper semi-continuous on E, so that $\{x \in E : f(x) \leqslant \alpha\}$ is closed and $\{x \in E : f(x) > \alpha\}$ is open for any $\alpha \in \mathbf{R}$.

2.28 Exercise
Let $E \subset \mathbf{R}^m$ and let $f : E \to \mathbf{R}$. Then f is continuous on E if and only if f is both upper and lower semi-continuous.

2.29 Theorem
Let $K \subset \mathbf{R}^m$ be compact and let $f : K \to \mathbf{R}$. If f is upper semi-continuous (resp. lower semi-continuous) then f achieves its maximum (resp. minimum) on K.

2.30 Proof
We will prove the result only for upper semi-continuity. Clearly $\{\{x \in K : f(x) < \alpha\} : \alpha \in \mathbf{R}\}$ is an open cover of K and so has a finite subcover. Since these sets are nested, f is bounded above on K. Let $\alpha = \sup_{x \in K} f(x)$. Then for each n, $\{x \in K : f(x) \geqslant \alpha - \frac{1}{n}\}$ is a nonempty closed subset of K. This family clearly has the finite

intersection property; and since K is compact, the intersection of the entire family is nonempty. (Rudin [1976, 2.36]). Thus $\{x : f(x) = \alpha\}$ is nonempty.

2.31 Definition
Let $E \subset X$. The *indicator function* (or *characteristic function*) of E is the function $f : X \to \mathbf{R}$ defined by $f(x) = 1$ if $x \in E$, and $f(x) = 0$ if $x \notin E$.

2.32 Exercise
Let $E \subset X \subset \mathbf{R}^m$. If E is closed in X, the indicator function of E is upper semi-continuous on X; and if E is open in X, the indicator function of E is lower semi-continuous on X.

2.33 Remark
The following definition of asymptotic cone is not the usual one, but agrees with the usual definition for closed convex sets. (See Rockafellar [1970, Theorem 8.2].) This definition was chosen because it makes most properties of asymptotic cones trivial consequences of the definition. Intuitively, the asymptotic cone of a closed convex set is the set of all directions in which the set is unbounded.

2.34 Definition
Let $E \subset \mathbf{R}^m$. The *asymptotic cone* of E, denoted $\mathrm{A}E$ is the set of all possible limits of sequences of the form $\{\lambda_n x^n\}$, where each $x^n \in E$ and $\lambda_n \downarrow 0$.

2.35 Exercise
(a) $\mathrm{A}E$ is indeed a cone.
(b) If $E \subset F$, then $\mathrm{A}E \subset \mathrm{A}F$.
(c) $\mathrm{A}(E + x) = \mathrm{A}E$ for any $x \in \mathbf{R}^m$.
(d) $\mathrm{A}E_1 \subset \mathrm{A}(E_1 + E_2)$. Hint: Use (b).
(e) $\mathrm{A}\prod_{i \in I} E_i \subset \prod_{i \in I} \mathrm{A}E_i$.
(f) $\mathrm{A}E$ is closed.
(g) If E is convex, then $\mathrm{A}E$ is convex.
(h) If E is closed and convex, then $x + \mathrm{A}E \subset E$ for every $x \in E$. Hint: By (b) it suffices to show that if E is closed and convex and $0 \in E$, then $\mathrm{A}E \subset E$.
(i) If E contains the cone C, then $\mathrm{A}E \supset C$.
(j) $\mathrm{A}\bigcap_{i \in I} E_i \subset \bigcap_{i \in I} \mathrm{A}E_i$.

2.36 Proposition
A set $E \subset \mathbf{R}^m$ is bounded if and only if $\mathrm{A}E = \{0\}$.

2.37 Proof

If E is bounded, clearly $\mathbf{A}E = \{0\}$. If E is not bounded let $\{x^n\}$ be an unbounded sequence in E. Then $\lambda_n = |x^n|^{-1} \downarrow 0$ and $\{\lambda_n x^n\}$ is a sequence on the unit sphere, which is compact. Thus there is a subsequence converging to some x in the unit sphere. Such an x is a nonzero member of $\mathbf{A}E$.

2.38 Proposition

Let $E,F \subset \mathbf{R}^m$ be closed and nonempty. Suppose that $x \in \mathbf{A}E$, $y \in \mathbf{A}F$ and $x + y = 0$ together imply that $x = y = 0$. Then $E + F$ is closed.

2.39 Proof

Suppose $E + F$ is not closed. Then there is a sequence $\{x^n + y^n\} \subset E + F$ with $\{x^n\} \subset E$, $\{y^n\} \subset F$, and $x^n + y^n \rightarrow z \notin E + F$. Without loss of generality we may take $z = 0$, simply by translating E or F. (By 2.35b, this involves no loss of generality.) Neither sequence $\{x^n\}$ nor $\{y^n\}$ is bounded: For suppose $\{x^n\}$ were bounded. Since E is closed, there would be a subsequence of $\{x^n\}$ converging to $x \in E$. Then along that subsequence $y^n = -x^n$ converges to $-x$. Since F is closed, $-x \in F$, and so $0 \in E + F$, a contradiction.

Thus without loss of generality we can find a subsequence $\{x^n + y^n\}$ such that $x^n + y^n \rightarrow 0$, $|x^n| \rightarrow \infty$ and also that $\dfrac{x^n}{|x^n|} \rightarrow x$ and $\dfrac{y^n}{|y^n|} \rightarrow y$. We can make this last assumption because the unit sphere is compact.

Suppose that $x + y \neq 0$. Since x and y are on the unit sphere we have then that $0 \notin co\ \{x,y\}$. By 2.9 there is a $p \neq 0$ and a $c > 0$ such that $p \cdot x \geqslant c$ and $p \cdot y \geqslant c$. Now

$$p \cdot (x^n + y^n) = p \cdot x^n + p \cdot y^n = |x^n| p \cdot \frac{x^n}{|x^n|} + |y^n| p \cdot \frac{y^n}{|y^n|}.$$

Since $p \cdot \dfrac{x^n}{|x^n|} \rightarrow p \cdot x \geqslant c$, $p \cdot \dfrac{y^n}{|y^n|} \rightarrow p \cdot y \geqslant c$ and $|x^n| \rightarrow \infty$, we have $p \cdot (x^n + y^n) \rightarrow \infty$. But $x^n + y^n \rightarrow 0$, so $p \cdot (x^n + y^n) \rightarrow 0$, a contradiction. Thus $x + y = 0$.

But $x \in \mathbf{A}E$ and $y \in \mathbf{A}F$ and since x and y are on the unit sphere they are nonzero. The proposition follows by contraposition.

2.40 Definition

Let $C_1,\ldots,C_n$ be cones in $\mathbf{R}^m$. We say that they are *positively semi-independent* if whenever $x^i \in C_i$ for each i and $\sum_i x^i = 0$, then $x^1 = \ldots = x^n = 0$. Clearly, any subset of a set of semi-independent cones is also semi-independent.

2.41 Corollary

Let $E_i \subset \mathbf{R}^m$, $i = 1,\ldots,n$, be closed and nonempty. If $\mathrm{A}E_i$, $i = 1,\ldots,n$, are positively semi-independent, then $\sum_{i=1}^{n} E_i$ is closed.

2.42 Proof

This follows from Proposition 2.38 by induction on n.

2.43 Corollary

Let $E,F \subset \mathbf{R}^m$ be closed and let F be compact. Then $E + F$ is closed.

2.44 Proof

A compact set is bounded, so by 2.36 its asymptotic cone is $\{0\}$. Apply Proposition 2.38.

CHAPTER 3

Simplexes

3.0 Note

Simplexes are the simplest of convex sets. For this reason we often prove theorems first for the case of simplexes and then extend the results to more general convex sets. One nice feature of simplexes is that all simplexes with the same number of vertexes are isomorphic. There are two commonly used definitions of a simplex. The one we use here follows Kuratowski [1972] and makes simplexes open sets. The other definition corresponds to what we call closed simplexes.

3.1 Definition

A set $\{x^0,...,x^n\} \subset \mathbf{R}^m$ is *affinely independent* if $\sum_{i=0}^{n} \lambda_i x^i = 0$ and $\sum_{i=0}^{n} \lambda_i = 0$ imply that $\lambda_0 = ... = \lambda_n = 0$.

3.2 Exercise

If $\{x^0,...,x^n\} \subset \mathbf{R}^m$ is affinely independent, then $m \geqslant n$.

3.3 Definition

An *n-simplex* is the set of all strictly positive convex combinations of an $n+1$ element affinely independent set. A *closed n-simplex* is the convex hull of an affinely independent set of $n+1$ vectors. The simplex $x^0 \cdots x^n$ (written without commas) is the set of all strictly positive convex combinations of the x^i vectors, i.e.,

$$x^0 \cdots x^n = \left\{ \sum_{i=0}^{n} \lambda_i x^i : \lambda_i > 0,\ i = 0,...,n;\ \sum_{i=0}^{n} \lambda_i = 1 \right\}.$$

Each x^i is a *vertex* of $x^0...x^n$ and each k-simplex $x^{i_0}...x^{i_k}$ is a *face* of $x^0 \cdots x^n$. By this definition each vertex is a face and $x^0 \cdots x^n$ is a face of itself. It is easy to see that the closure of $x^0 \cdots x^n = co\ \{x^0,...,x^n\}$. For $y = \sum_{i=0}^{n} \lambda_i x^i \in co\ \{x^0,...,x^n\}$, let $\chi(y) = \{i : \lambda_i > 0\}$. If $\chi(y) = \{i_0,...,i_k\}$, then $y \in x^{i_0} \cdots x^{i_k}$. This face is called the *carrier* of y. It follows that the union of all the faces of $x^0 \cdots x^n$ is its closure.

3.4 Exercise
If y belongs to the convex hull of the affinely independent set $\{x^0,...,x^n\}$, there is a unique set of numbers $\lambda_0, \ldots, \lambda_n$ such that $y = \sum_{i=0}^{n} \lambda_i x^i$. Consequently y belongs to exactly one face of $x^0...x^n$. This means that the concept of carrier described above is well-defined. The numbers $\lambda_0, \ldots, \lambda_n$ are called the *barycentric coordinates* of y.

3.5 Definition
The *standard n-simplex* is
$\{y \in \mathbf{R}^{n+1} : y_i > 0,\ i = 0,...,n;\ \sum_{i=0}^{n} y_i = 1\} = e^0 \cdots e^n$. Let Δ_n denote the closure of the standard n-simplex, which we call the *standard closed n-simplex*. (We may simply write Δ when n is apparent from the context.)

3.6 Exercise
The reason $e^0 \cdots e^n \subset \mathbf{R}^{n+1}$ is called the standard n-simplex is a result of the following. Let $T = x^0 \cdots x^n \subset \mathbf{R}^m$ be an n-simplex. Define the mapping $\sigma : \Delta \to \overline{T}$ by $\sigma(y) = \sum_{i=0}^{n} y_i x^i$. Then σ is bijective and continuous and σ^{-1} is continuous. For $x \in \overline{T}$, $\sigma^{-1}(x)$ is the vector of barycentric coordinates of x.

3.7 Exercise
Let $x,z \in \Delta$. If $x \leqslant z$, then $x = z$.

3.8 Definition
Let $T = x^0...x^n$ be an n-simplex. A *simplicial subdivision* of $\overline{T}$ is a finite collection of simplexes $\{T_i : i \in I\}$ satisfying $\bigcup_{i \in I} T_i = \overline{T}$ and such that for any $i,j \in I$, $\overline{T}_j \cap \overline{T}_i$ is either empty or equal to the closure of a common face. The *mesh* of a subdivision is the diameter of the largest subsimplex.

3.9 Example
Refer to Figure 3(a). The collection

$$\{x^0x^2x^4, x^1x^2x^3, x^1x^3x^4, x^0x^2, x^0x^4, x^1x^2, x^1x^3,$$
$$x^1x^4, x^2x^3, x^3x^4, x^0, x^1, x^2, x^3, x^4\}$$

indicated by the solid lines is *not* a simplicial subdivision of $cl\ x^0x^1x^2$. This is because $cl\ x^0x^2x^4 \cap cl\ x^1x^2x^3 = cl\ x^2x^3$, which is not the

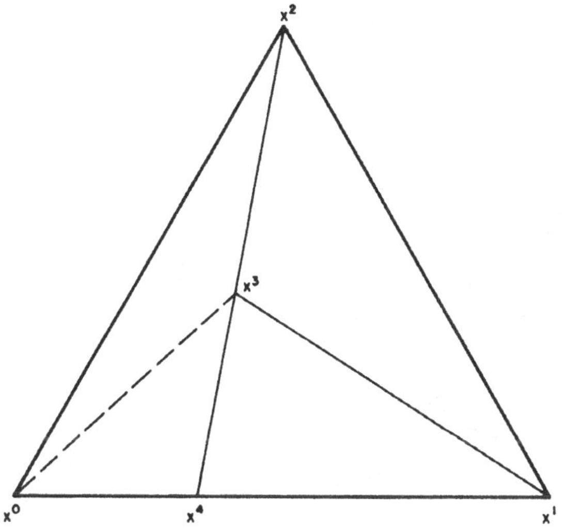

Figure 3(a)

closure of a face of $x^0x^2x^4$. By replacing $x^0x^2x^4$ by $x^0x^2x^3$, $x^0x^3x^4$ and x^0x^3 as indicated by the dotted line, the result is a valid simplicial subdivision.

3.10 Example: Equilateral Subdivision

For any positive integer m, the set

$$V = \{v \in \mathbf{R}_+^{n+1} : v_i = k_i/m,\ i = 0,\ldots,n;\ \sum_{i=0}^{n} k_i = m;\ k_i \textit{ integers},\ i = 0,\ldots,n\}$$

is the set of vertexes of a simplicial subdivision of Δ_n. See Figure 3(b). This subdivision has m^n n-simplexes of diameter $\frac{\sqrt{2}}{m}$ and assorted lower dimensional simplexes. This example shows that there are subdivisions of arbitrarily small mesh.

3.11 Example: Barycentric Subdivision

For any simplex $T = x^0 \ldots x^n$, the *barycenter* of T, denoted $b(T)$, is the point $\frac{1}{n+1} \sum_{i=0}^{n} x^i$. For simplexes T_1, T_2 define $T_1 > T_2$ to mean T_2 is a face of T_1 and $T_1 \neq T_2$. Given a simplex T, the family of all simplexes $b(T_0) \ldots b(T_k)$ such that $T \geqslant T_0 > T_1 > \ldots > T_k$ is a simplicial subdivision of T called the *first barycentric subdivision* of T. See Figure 3(c). Further barycentric subdivisions are defined recursively. It can be shown that there are barycentric subdivisions of arbitrarily small mesh.

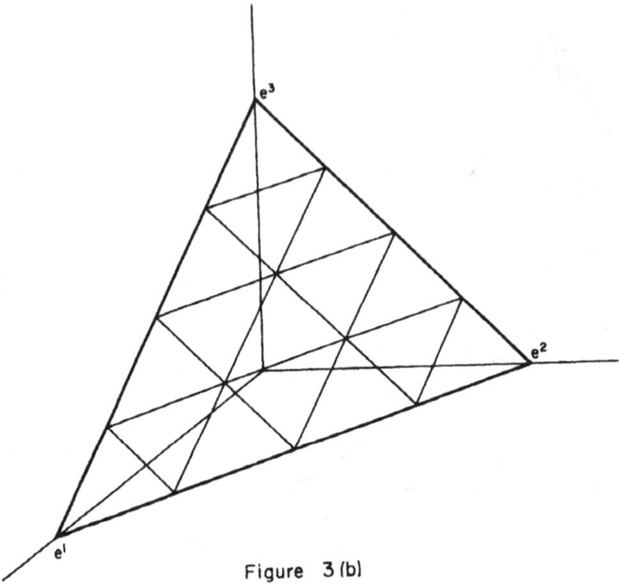

Figure 3(b)

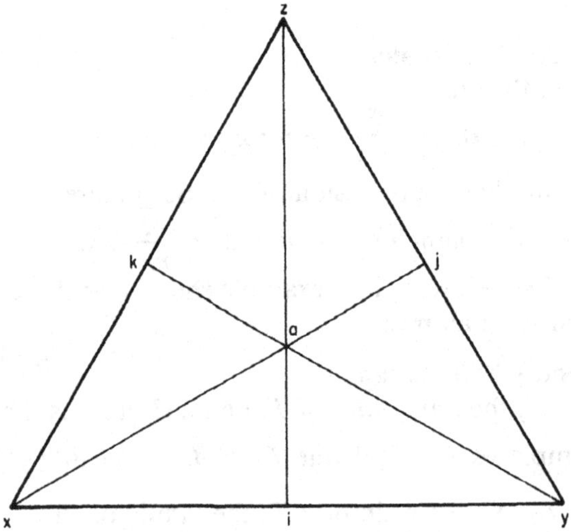

Figure 3(c)

CHAPTER 4

Sperner's lemma

4.0 Definition
Let $\overline{T} = cl\, x^0 \cdots x^n$ be simplicially subdivided. Let V denote the collection of all the vertexes of all the subsimplexes. (Note that each $x^i \in V$.) A function $\lambda : V \rightarrow \{0,...,n\}$ satisfying

$$\lambda(v) \in \chi(v)$$

is called a *proper labeling* of the subdivision. (Recall the definition of the carrier χ from 3.3.) Call a subsimplex *completely labeled* if λ assumes all the values $0,...,n$ on its set of vertexes.

4.1 Theorem (Sperner [1928])
Let $\overline{T} = cl\, x^0 \cdots x^n$ be simplicially subdivided and properly labeled by the function λ. Then there are an odd number of completely labeled subsimplexes in the subdivision.

4.2 Proof (Kuhn [1968])
The proof is by induction on n. The case $n = 0$ is trivial. The simplex consists of a single point x^0, which must bear the label 0, and so there is one completely labeled subsimplex, x^0 itself.

We now assume the statement to be true for $n-1$ and prove it for n. Let

- C denote the set of all completely labeled n-simplexes;
- A denote the set of almost completely labeled n-simplexes, i.e., those such that the range of λ is exactly $\{0,...,n-1\}$;
- B denote the set of $(n-1)$-simplexes on the boundary which bear all the labels $\{0,...,n-1\}$; and
- E denote the set of all $(n-1)$-simplexes which bear all the labels $\{0,...,n-1\}$.

An $n-1$ simplex either lies on the boundary and is the face of a single n-simplex in the subdivision or it is a common face of two n-simplexes. We can view this situation as a graph, i.e., a collection of nodes and edges joining them. Let $D = C \cup A \cup B$ be the set of nodes and E the set of edges. Define edge $e \in E$ and node $d \in D$ to

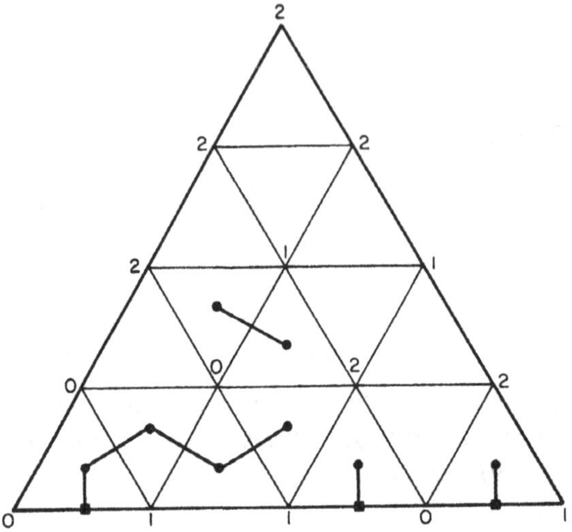

Figure 4

be *incident* if either

(i) $d \in A \cup C$ and e is a face of d or

(ii) $e = d \in B$.

See Figure 4 for an example.

The *degree* of a node d, $\delta(d)$, is the number of edges incident at d. If $d \in A$, then one label is repeated and exactly two faces of d belong to E, so its degree is 2. The degree of $d \in B \cup C$ is 1. On the other hand, each edge is incident at exactly two nodes: If an $(n-1)$-simplex lies on the boundary and bears labels $\{0,\ldots,n-1\}$, then it is incident at itself (as a node in B) and at an n-simplex (which must be a node in either A or C). If an $(n-1)$-simplex is a common face of two n-simplexes, then each n-simplex belongs to either A or C.

Thus

$$\delta(d) = \begin{cases} 1 & d \in B \cup C \\ 2 & d \in A \end{cases}$$

A standard graph theoretic argument yields $\sum_{d \in D} \delta(d) = 2|E|$. That is, since each edge joins exactly two nodes, counting the number of edges incident at each node and adding them up counts each edge twice. By the definition of δ, $\sum_{d \in D} \delta(d) = 2|A| + |B| + |C|$. Thus $2|E| = 2|A| + |B| + |C|$ so that $|B| + |C|$ is even. Since $|B|$ is odd by the induction hypothesis, we must have that $|C|$ is odd.

4.3 Remarks

Theorem 4.1 is known as Sperner's lemma. The importance of the theorem is as an existence theorem. Zero is not an odd number, so there exists at least one completely labeled subsimplex. The value of finding a completely labeled subsimplex as an approximate solution to various fixed point or other problems is discussed in Chapter 10. It should be noted that there is a stronger statement of Sperner's lemma. It turns out that the number of completely labeled subsimplexes with the same orientation as T is exactly one more than the number of subsimplexes with the opposite orientation. The general notion of orientation is beyond the scope of these notes, but in two dimensions is easily explained. A two-dimensional completely labeled subsimplex will carry the labels 0,1,2. The orientation is determined by whether the labels occur in this order counting clockwise or counter-clockwise. For a proof of this "superstrong" form of Sperner's lemma, as well as related combinatorial results, see Le Van [1982].

CHAPTER 5

The Knaster-Kuratowski-Mazurkiewicz lemma

5.0 Remark

The K-K-M lemma (Corollary 5.4) is quite basic and in some ways more useful than Brouwer's fixed point theorem, although the two are equivalent.

5.1 Theorem (Knaster-Kuratowski-Mazurkiewicz [1929])

Let $\Delta = co\ \{e^0, \ldots, e^m\} \subset \mathbf{R}^{m+1}$ and let $\{F_0, \ldots, F_m\}$ be a family of closed subsets of Δ such that for every $A \subset \{0,...,m\}$ we have

$$co\ \{e^i : i \in A\} \subset \bigcup_{i \in A} F_i. \qquad 5.2$$

Then $\bigcap_{i=0}^{m} F_i$ is compact and nonempty.

5.3 Proof (Knaster-Kuratowski-Mazurkiewicz [1929])

The intersection is clearly compact, being a closed subset of a compact set. Let $\varepsilon > 0$ be given and subdivide Δ into subsimplexes of diameter $\leqslant \varepsilon$. (See 3.10 for example.) For a vertex v of the subdivision belonging to the face $e^{i_0} \cdots e^{i_k}$, by 5.2 there is some index i in $\{i_0, \ldots, i_k\}$ with $v \in F_i$. If we label all the vertexes this way, then the labeling satisfies the hypotheses of Sperner's lemma so there is a completely labeled subsimplex ${}^{\varepsilon}p^0 \cdots {}^{\varepsilon}p^m$, with ${}^{\varepsilon}p^i \in F_i$ for each i. As $\varepsilon \downarrow 0$, choose a convergent subsequence ${}^{\varepsilon}p^i \rightarrow z$. Since F_i is closed and ${}^{\varepsilon}p^i \in F_i$ for each i, we have $z \in \bigcap_{i=0}^{m} F_i$.

5.4 Corollary

Let $K = co\ \{a^0, \ldots, a^m\} \subset \mathbf{R}^k$ and let $\{F_0, \ldots, F_m\}$ be a family of closed sets such that for every $A \subset \{0,...,m\}$ we have

$$co\ \{a^i : i \in A\} \subset \bigcup_{i \in A} F_i. \qquad 5.5$$

Then $K \cap \bigcap_{i=0}^{m} F_i$ is compact and nonempty.

5.6 Proof

Again compactness is immediate. Define the mapping $\sigma : \Delta \to K$ by $\sigma(z) = \sum_{i=0}^{m} z_i a^i$. If $\{a^0, \ldots, a^m\}$ is not an affinely independent set, then σ is not injective, but it is nevertheless continuous. Put $E_i = \sigma^{-1}[F_i \cap K]$ for each i. Since σ is continuous, each E_i is a closed subset of Δ. It is straightforward to verify that 5.2 is satisfied by $\{E_0, \ldots, E_m\}$ and so let $z \in \bigcap_{i=0}^{m} E_i \neq \varnothing$. Then $\sigma(z) \in \bigcap_{i=0}^{m} F_i \neq \varnothing$.

5.7 Corollary (Fan [1961])

Let $X \subset \mathbf{R}^m$, and for each $x \in X$ let $F(x) \subset \mathbf{R}^m$ be closed. Suppose:

(i) For any finite subset $\{x^1, \ldots, x^k\} \subset X$,

$$co\,\{x^1, \ldots, x^k\} \subset \bigcup_{i=1}^{k} F(x^i).$$

(ii) $F(x)$ is compact for some $x \in X$.

Then $\bigcap_{x \in X} F(x)$ is compact and nonempty.

5.8 Proof

The conclusion follows from Corollary 5.4 and the fact that in a compact set, a family of closed sets with the finite intersection property has a nonempty intersection. (Rudin [1976, 2.36].)

CHAPTER 6

Brouwer's fixed point theorem

6.0 Remark

The basic fixed point theorem that we will use is due to Brouwer [1912]. For our purposes the most useful form of Brouwer's fixed point theorem is Corollary 6.6 below, but the simplest version to prove is Theorem 6.1.

6.1 Theorem

Let $f : \Delta_m \to \Delta_m$ be continuous. Then f has a fixed point.

6.2 Proof

Let $\varepsilon > 0$ be given and subdivide Δ simplicially into subsimplexes of diameter $\leqslant \varepsilon$. Let V be the set of vertexes of the subdivision and define a labeling function $\lambda : V \to \{0,...,m\}$ as follows. For $v \in x^{i_0}...x^{i_k}$ choose

$$\lambda(v) \in \{i_0, \ldots, i_k\} \cap \{i : f_i(v) \leqslant v_i\}.$$

(This intersection is nonempty, for if $f_i(v) > v_i$ for all $i \in \{i_0, \ldots, i_k\}$, we would have

$$1 = \sum_{i=0}^{m} f_i(v) > \sum_{j=0}^{k} v_{i_j} = \sum_{i=0}^{m} v_i = 1,$$

a contradiction, where the second equality follows from $v \in x^{i_0} \cdots x^{i_k}$.) Since λ so defined satisfies the hypotheses of Sperner's lemma (4.1), there exists a completely labeled subsimplex. That is, there is a simplex ${}^{\varepsilon}p^0 \cdots {}^{\varepsilon}p^m$ such that $f_i({}^{\varepsilon}p^i) \leqslant {}^{\varepsilon}p^i_i$ for each i. Letting $\varepsilon \downarrow 0$ we can extract a convergent subsequence (as Δ is compact) of simplexes such that ${}^{\varepsilon}p^i \to z$ as $\varepsilon \to 0$ for all $i = 0,...,m$. Since f is continuous we must have $f_i(z) \leqslant z_i$, $i = 0,...,m$, so by 3.7, $f(z) = z$.

6.3 Definition

A set A is *homeomorphic* to the set B if there is a bijective continuous function $h : A \to B$ such that h^{-1} is also continuous. Such a function h is called a *homeomorphism*.

6.4 Corollary
Let K be homeomorphic to Δ and let $f : K \to K$ be continuous. Then f has a fixed point.

6.5 Proof
Let $h : \Delta \to K$ be a homeomorphism. Then $h^{-1} \circ f \circ h : \Delta \to \Delta$ is continuous, so there exists z' with $h^{-1} \circ f \circ h(z') = z'$. Set $z = h(z')$. Then $h^{-1}(f(z)) = h^{-1}(z)$, so $f(z) = z$ as h is injective.

6.6 Corollary
Let $K \subset \mathbf{R}^m$ be convex and compact and let $f : K \to K$ be continuous. Then f has a fixed point.

6.7 Proof
Since K is compact, it is contained in some sufficiently large simplex T. Define $h : T \to K$ by setting $h(x)$ equal to the point in K closest to x. By 2.7, h is continuous and is equal to the identity on K. So $f \circ h : T \to K \subset T$ has a fixed point z. Such a fixed point cannot belong to $T \setminus K$, as $f \circ h$ maps into K. Thus $z \in K$ and $f \circ h(z) = z$; but $h(z) = z$, so $f(z) = z$.

6.8 Note
The above method of proof provides a somewhat more general theorem. Following Borsuk [1967], we say that E is an *r-image* of F if there are continuous functions $h : F \to E$ and $g : E \to F$ such that $h \circ g$ is the identity on E. Such a function h is called an *r-map* of F onto E. In particular, if h is a homeomorphism, then it is an r-map. In the special case where $E \subset F$ and g is the inclusion map, i.e., the identity map on E, we say that E is a *retract* of F and that h is a *retraction.*

6.9 Theorem
Let E be an r-image of a compact convex set $K \subset \mathbf{R}^m$, and let $f : E \to E$ be continuous. Then f has a fixed point.

6.10 Proof
The map $g \circ f \circ h : K \to K$ has a fixed point z, $(g \circ f)(h(z)) = z$. Set $x = h(z) \in E$. Then $(g \circ f)(x) = z$, so $h \circ g \circ f(x) = h(z) = x$, but $h \circ g$ is the identity on E, so $f(x) = x$.

6.11 Remark
Let B_m be the unit ball in $\mathbf{R}^m$, i.e., $B_m = \{x \in \mathbf{R}^m : |x| \leqslant 1\}$, and let $\partial B_m = \{x \in \mathbf{R}^m : |x| = 1\}$. The following theorem is equivalent to the fixed point theorem.

6.12 Theorem
∂B_m is not an r-image of B_m.

6.13 Proof

Suppose ∂B is an r-image of B. Then there are continuous functions $g : \partial B \to B$ and $h : B \to \partial B$ such that $h \circ g$ is the identity. Define $f(x) = g(-h(x))$. Then f is continuous and maps B into itself and so by 6.6 has a fixed point z. That is, $z = g(-h(z))$ and so $h(z) = (h \circ g)(-h(z)) = -h(z)$. Thus $h(z) = 0 \notin \partial B$, a contradiction.

6.14 Exercise: Theorem 6.12 implies the fixed point theorem for balls

Hint: Let $f : B \to B$ be continuous and suppose that f has no fixed point. For each x let $\lambda(x) = \max \{\lambda : |x + \lambda(f(x) - x)| = 1\}$ and put $h(x) = x + \lambda(x)(f(x) - x)$. Then h is an r-map of B onto ∂B.

6.15 Note

For any continuous function $f : E \to \mathbf{R}^m$, the set of fixed points $\{x : x = f(x)\}$ is a closed (but possibly empty) subset of E. If E is compact, then the set of fixed points is also compact.

CHAPTER 7

Maximization of binary relations

7.0 Remark

The following theorems give sufficient conditions for a binary relation to have a maximal element on a compact set, and are of interest as purely mathematical results. They also allow us to extend the classical results of equilibrium theory to cover consumers whose preferences may not be representable by utility functions.

The problem faced by a consumer is to choose a consumption pattern given his income and prevailing prices. Let there be m commodities. Prices are given by a vector $p \in \mathbf{R}^m$. If the consumer's consumption set is $X \subset \mathbf{R}^m$, then the set of commodity vectors available to the consumer is $\{x \in X : p \cdot x \leqslant M\}$, where M is the consumer's income. An important feature of the budget set is that it is positively homogeneous of degree zero in prices and income. That is, it remains unchanged if the price vector and income are multiplied by the same positive number. If $X = \mathbf{R}^m_+$ and $p > 0$, then the budget set is compact. If some prices are allowed to be zero, then the budget set is no longer compact. It can be compactified by setting some arbitrary upper bound on consumption. If this bound is large enough it will have no effect on the equilibria of the economy. (See Chapter 20.) Under these conditions, if the consumer's preferences are representable by a continuous utility function u (i.e., the consumer weakly prefers x to y if and only if $u(x) \geqslant u(y)$), then a classical theorem of Weierstrass (Rudin [1976, 4.16]; cf. 2.29) states that u will achieve a maximum on the budget set. The set of maximal vectors in the budget set is called the consumer's demand set. In Chapter 11 notions are introduced as to what it means to say that the demand set varies continuously with respect to changes in prices and income. In this chapter some of the conditions on the preferences are relaxed, while still ensuring that the demand set is nonempty.

The preference relation U is taken to be primitive. For each x, $U(x)$ is the set of alternatives that are strictly preferred to x. This set is sometimes called the *upper contour set* of x. Define $U^{-1}(x) = \{y : x \in U(y)\}$, the *lower contour set* of x. A *U-maximal* element x satisfies $U(x) = \emptyset$.

Assuming that the consumer's preferences are representable by a continuous utility ensures a number of things. Setting $U(x) = \{y : u(y) > u(x)\}$, then $U^{-1}(x) = \{y : u(y) < u(x)\}$, and $y \notin U(x)$ means $u(x) \geq u(y)$. The continuity of u implies that $U(x)$ and $U^{-1}(x)$ are open for each x and that $\{(x,y) : y \in U(x)\}$ is open. The preferences are also *transitive*. That is, if $x \notin U(y)$ and $y \notin U(z)$, then $x \notin U(z)$. Both of these consequences have been criticized as being unrealistically strong. Fortunately, they are not necessary to showing that the demand set is nonempty. There are two basic approaches to showing nonemptiness of the demand set without assuming transitivity of preferences. The first was developed by Fan [1961], Sonnenschein [1971], Shafer [1974] and Shafer and Sonnenschein [1975], the other may be found in Sloss [1971], Brown [1973], Bergstrom [1975] and Walker [1977].

Fan [1961, Lemma 4] does not phrase his results in terms of maximizing binary relations, but his results can be interpreted that way. Fan assumes that U has an open graph, that $U(x)$ is convex, and that U is irreflexive, i.e., $x \notin U(x)$. Sonnenschein [1971] weakens the openness assumption, assuming only that $U^{-1}(x)$ is open for each x. Arrow [1969] applies Sonnenschein's theorem to the problem of existence of equilibrium in a political model. Shafer [1974] constructs real-valued functions for analyzing such relations. Both Sonnenschein and Shafer assume that preferences are complete, and work with a weak preference relation as the underlying source of the strict preference. This involves no loss of generality, as a strict preference may be converted into a complete weak preference relation by making any noncomparable elements indifferent. This creates no problems because we do not require indifference to be transitive. Shafer and Sonnenschein [1975] weaken the convexity condition and combine it with irreflexivity by assuming only that $x \notin co\ U(x)$. This assumption is closely related to Sloss' [1971] assumption of *directionality*. A binary relation is directional if for each x, there is p such that $p \cdot z > p \cdot x$ for all $z \in U(x)$. If $cl\ U(x)$ is contained in some open half space, then the Shafer-Sonnenschein assumption implies directionality. (This follows from the separating hyperplane theorem (2.9).) Theorem 7.2 below is a refinement of this approach. Following Shafer and Sonnenschein, it assumes that $x \notin co\ U(x)$, but not all the lower contour sets are assumed to be open. Sonnenschein [1971] gives an example that indicates that preferences of this form are indeed a generalization of preferences studied in classical demand theory. That is, these assumptions do not imply transitivity.

The second approach involves no convexity assumptions, but uses the notion of *acyclicity*. The preference U is acyclic if $x^2 \in U(x^1), x^3 \in U(x^2), \ldots, x^n \in U(x^{n-l})$ implies that $x^1 \notin U(x^n)$. (In particular, $x \notin U(x)$.) It is clear that an acyclic relation will always have a maximal element on a finite set. If the lower contour sets are open, then a compact set has maximal elements. Unlike the first approach, no fixed point or related techniques are required to prove this theorem.

Both theorems can be extended to cover binary relations on sets which are not compact, by imposing assumptions on the relation outside of some compact set. This is done in Proposition 7.8 and Theorem 7.10.

7.1 Definition

A *binary relation* U on a set K associates to each $x \in K$ a set $U(x) \subset K$, which may be interpreted as the set of those objects in K that are "better" "larger" or "after" x. Define $U^{-1}(x) = \{y \in K : x \in U(y)\}$. An element $x \in K$ is *U-maximal* if $U(x) = \emptyset$. The *U-maximal set* is $\{x \in K : U(x) = \emptyset\}$. The *graph* of U is $\{(x,y) : y \in U(x)\}$.

7.2 Theorem (cf. Sonnenschein [1971])

Let $K \subset \mathbf{R}^m$ be compact and convex and let U be a relation on K satisfying the following:

(i) $x \notin co\ U(x)$ for all $x \in K$.

(ii) if $y \in U^{-1}(x)$, then there exists some $x' \in K$ (possibly $x'=x$) such that $y \in int\ U^{-1}(x')$.

Then K has a U-maximal element, and the U-maximal set is compact.

7.3 Proof (cf. Fan [1961, Lemma 4]; Sonnenschein [1971, Theorem 4])

Note that $\{x : U(x) = \emptyset\}$ is just $\bigcap_{x \in K} (K \setminus U^{-1}(x))$. By hypothesis (ii),

$$\bigcap_{x \in K} (K \setminus U^{-1}(x)) = \bigcap_{x' \in K} (K \setminus int\ U^{-1}(x')).$$

This latter intersection is clearly compact, being the intersection of compact sets.

For each x, put $F(x) = K \setminus (int\ U^{-1}(x))$. As noted above, each $F(x)$ is compact. If $y \in co\ \{x^i : i = 1,\ldots,n\}$, then $y \in \bigcup_{i=1}^{n} F(x^i)$: Suppose that $y \notin \bigcup_{i=1}^{n} F(x^i)$. Then $y \in U^{-1}(x^i)$ for all i, so $x^i \in U(y)$ for all i. But then $y \in co\ \{x^i\} \subset co\ U(y)$, which violates (i). It then follows from the Knaster-Kuratowski-Mazurkiewicz lemma as extended by Fan (5.7) that $\bigcap_{x \in K} F(x) \neq \emptyset$.

7.4 Corollary (Fan's Lemma [1961, Lemma 4])
Let $K \subset \mathbf{R}^m$ be compact and convex. Let $E \subset K \times K$ be closed and suppose

(i) $(x,x) \in E$ for all $x \in K$.
(ii) for each $y \in K$, $\{x \in K : (x,y) \notin E\}$ is convex (possibly empty).

Then there exists $\bar{y} \in K$ such that $K \times \{\bar{y}\} \subset E$. The set of such $\bar{y}$ is compact.

7.5 Corollary (Fan's Lemma -- Alternate Statement)
Let $K \subset \mathbf{R}^m$ be compact and let U be a relation on K satisfying:

(i) $x \notin U(x)$ for all $x \in K$.
(ii) $U(x)$ is convex for all $x \in K$.
(iii) $\{(x,y) : y \in U(x)\}$ is open in $K \times K$.

Then the U-maximal set is compact and nonempty.

7.6 Exercise
Show that both statements of Fan's lemma are special cases of Theorem 7.2.

7.7 Definition
A set $C \subset \mathbf{R}^m$ is called *σ-compact* if there is a sequence $\{C_n\}$ of compact subsets of C satisfying $\bigcup_n C_n = C$. The euclidean space $\mathbf{R}^m$ is itself σ-compact as $\mathbf{R}^m = \bigcup_n \{x : |x| \leqslant n\}$. So is any closed convex cone in $\mathbf{R}^m$. Another example is the open unit ball,
$\{x : |x| < 1\} = \bigcup_n \{x : |x| \leqslant 1 - \frac{1}{n}\}$.

Let $C = \bigcup_n C_n$, where $\{C_n\}$ is an increasing sequence of nonempty compact sets. A sequence $\{x^k\}$ is said to be *escaping from C* (relative to $\{C_n\}$) if for each n there is an M such that for all $k \geqslant M$, $x^k \notin C_n$. A *boundary condition* on a binary relation on C puts restrictions on escaping sequences. Boundary conditions can be used to guarantee the existence of maximal elements for sets that are not compact. Theorems 7.8 and 7.10 below are two examples.

7.8 Proposition
Let $C \subset \mathbf{R}^m$ be convex and σ-compact and let U be a binary relation on C satisfying

(i) $x \notin co\ U(x)$ for all $x \in C$.
(ii) $U^{-1}(x)$ is open (in C) for each $x \in C$.

Let $D \subset C$ be compact and satisfy

(iii) for each $x \in C \setminus D$, there exists $z \in D$ with $z \in U(x)$.
Then C has a U-maximal element. The set of all U-maximal elements is a compact subset of D.

7.9 Proof

Since C is σ-compact, there is a sequence $\{C_n\}$ of compact subsets of C satisfying $\bigcup_n C_n = C$. Set $K_n = co\left[\bigcup_{j=1}^{n} C_j \cup D\right]$. Then $\{K_n\}$ is an increasing sequence of compact convex sets each containing D with $\bigcup_n K_n = C$. By Theorem 7.2, it follows from (i) and (ii) that each K_n has a U-maximal element x^n, i.e., $U(x^n) \cap K_n = \varnothing$. Since $D \subset K_n$, (iii) implies that $x^n \in D$. Since D is compact, we can extract a convergent subsequence $x^n \to \bar{x} \in D$.

Suppose that $U(\bar{x}) \neq \varnothing$. Let $z \in U(\bar{x})$. By (ii) there is a neighborhood W of $\bar{x}$ contained in $U^{-1}(z)$. For large enough n, $x^n \in W$ and $z \in K_n$. Thus $z \in U(x^n) \cap K_n$, contradicting the maximality of x^n. Thus $U(\bar{x}) = \varnothing$.

Hypothesis (iii) implies that any U-maximal element must belong to D, and (ii) implies that the U-maximal set is closed. Thus the U-maximal set is a compact subset of D.

7.10 Theorem

Let $C = \bigcup_n C_n$, where $\{C_n\}$ is an increasing sequence of nonempty compact convex subsets of $\mathbf{R}^m$. Let U be a binary relation on C satisfying the following:

(i) $x \notin co\, U(x)$ for all $x \in C$.
(ii) $U^{-1}(x)$ is open (in C) for each $x \in C$.
(iii) For each escaping sequence $\{x^n\}$, there is a $z \in C$ such that $z \in U(x^n)$ for infinitely many n.

Then C has a U-maximal element and the U-maximal set is a closed subset of C.

7.11 Proof

By 7.2 each C_n has a U-maximal element x^n, i.e., $U(x^n) \cap C_n = \varnothing$. Suppose the sequence $\{x^n\}$ were escaping from C. Then by the boundary condition (iii), there is a $z \in C$ such that $z \in U(x^n)$ infinitely often. But since $\{C_n\}$ is increasing, $z \in C_k$ for all sufficiently large k. Thus for infinitely many n, $z \in U(x^n) \cap C_k$, which contradicts the U-maximality of x^k. Thus $\{x^n\}$ is not escaping from C. This means that some subsequence of $\{x^n\}$ must lie entirely in some C_k, which is compact. Thus there is a subsequence of $\{x^n\}$ converging to some $\bar{x} \in C$.

This $\bar{x}$ is U-maximal: Let $x^n \to \bar{x}$ be a convergent subsequence and suppose that there exists some $y \in U(\bar{x})$. Then for sufficiently large k, $y \in C_k$, and by (ii) there is a neighborhood of $\bar{x}$ contained in $U^{-1}(y)$. So for large enough k, $y \in C_k \cap U(x^k)$, again contradicting the maximality of x^k. Thus $U(\bar{x}) = \varnothing$. The closedness of the U-maximal set follows from (ii).

7.12 Theorem (Sloss [1971], Brown [1973], Bergstrom [1975], Walker [1977])

Let $K \subset \mathbf{R}^m$ be compact, and let U be a relation on K satisfying the following:

(i) $x^2 \in U(x^1),\ldots,x^n \in U(x^{n-1}) \rightarrow x^1 \notin U(x^n)$ for all $x^1,\ldots,x^n \in K$.

(ii) $U^{-1}(x)$ is open for all $x \in K$.

Then the U-maximal set is compact and nonempty.

7.13 Proof (cf. Sloss [1971])

Suppose $U(x) \neq \varnothing$ for each x. Then as in the proof of 7.2, $\{U^{-1}(y) : y \in K\}$ is an open cover of K and so there is a finite subcover $\{U^{-1}(y^1),\ldots,U^{-1}(y^k)\}$. Since U is acyclic, the finite set $\{y^1,\ldots,y^k\}$ has a U-maximal element, say y^1. But then $y^1 \notin \bigcup_{i=1}^{k} U^{-1}(y^i)$, a contradiction. The proof of compactness of the U-maximal set is the same as in 7.2.

7.14 Exercise

Formulate and prove versions of Theorem 7.12 for σ-compact sets along the lines of Propositions 7.8 and 7.10.

7.15 Remark

It is trivial to observe that if for each x, $U'(x) \subset U(x)$, then $U(x) = \varnothing$ implies $U'(x) = \varnothing$. Nevertheless this observation is useful, as will be seen in 19.7. This motivates the following definition and results.

7.16 Definition

Let $K \subset \mathbf{R}^k$ be compact and convex and let U be a relation on K with open graph, i.e., such that $\{(x,y) : y \in U(x)\}$ is open, and satisfying $x \notin co\ U(x)$ for all x. Such a relation is called *FS*. (The FS is for Fan and Sonnenschein. This notion was first introduced by Borglin and Keiding [1976] under the name of KF [for Ky Fan].) Theorem 7.2 says that an FS relation must be empty-valued at some point. A relation μ on K is *locally FS-majorized* at x if there is a neighborhood V of x and an FS relation γ on K such that $\mu|_V$ is a *subrelation* of γ, i.e., for all $z \in V$, $\mu(z) \subset \gamma(z)$. A relation μ is *FS-majorized* if it is a subrelation of an FS relation.

7.17 Lemma

Let U be a relation on K that is everywhere locally FS-majorized, where $K \subset \mathbf{R}^m$ is compact and convex. Then U is FS-majorized.

7.18 Proof

For each x, let μ_x locally FS majorize U on the neighborhood V_x of x. Let $V_{x^1},...,V_{x^n}$ be a finite subcover of K and $F_1,...,F_n$ be a closed refinement, i.e., $F_i \subset V_i$ and $K \subset \bigcup_{i=1}^{n} F_i$. Define μ_i, $i = 1,...,n$ by

$$\mu_i(x) = \begin{cases} \mu_{x^i}(x) & x \in F_i \\ K & \text{otherwise.} \end{cases}$$

Define μ on K by $\mu(x) = \bigcap_{i=1}^{n} \mu_{x^i}(x)$. Then μ is FS and $U(x) \subset \mu(x)$ for all x.

7.19 Corollary to Theorem 7.2

Let U be everywhere locally FS-majorized. Then there is $x \in K$ with $U(x) = \varnothing$.

7.20 Proof

The result follows from 7.2 and 7.17.

CHAPTER 8

Variational inequalities, price equilibrium, and complementarity

8.0 Remarks

In this chapter we will examine two related problems, the equilibrium price problem and the complementarity problem. The equilibrium price problem is to find a price vector p which clears the markets for all commodities. The analysis in this chapter covers the case where the excess demand set is a singleton for each price vector and price vectors are nonnegative. The case of more general excess demand sets and price domains is taken up in Chapter 18. In the case at hand, given a price vector p, there is a vector $f(p)$ of excess demands for each commodity. We assume that f is a continuous function of p. (Conditions under which this is the case are discussed in Chapter 12.) A very important property of market excess demand functions is *Walras' law*. The mathematical statement of Walras' law can take either of two forms. The strong form of Walras' law is

$$p \cdot f(p) = 0 \quad \text{for all } p.$$

The weak form of Walras' law replaces the equality by the weak inequality $p \cdot f(p) \leqslant 0$. The economic meaning of Walras' law is that in a closed economy, at most all of everyone's income is spent, i.e., there is no net borrowing. To see how the mathematical statement follows from the economic statement, first consider a pure exchange economy. The ith consumer comes to market with vector w^i of commodities and leaves with a vector x^i of commodities. If all consumers face the price vector p, then their individual budgets require that $p \cdot x^i \leqslant p \cdot w^i$, that is, they cannot spend more than they earn. In this case, the excess demand vector $f(p)$ is just $\sum_i x^i - \sum_i w^i$, the sum of total demands minus the total supply. Summing up the individual budget constraints and rearranging terms yields $p \cdot f(p) \leqslant 0$, the weak form of Walras' law. The strong form obtains if each consumer spends all his income. The case of a production economy is similar. The jth supplier produces a net output vector y^j, which yields a net income of $p \cdot y^j$. In a private ownership economy this net income is redistributed to consumers. The new budget constraint from a consumer is that

$$p \cdot x^i \leqslant p \cdot w^i + \sum_j \alpha_j^i(p \cdot y^i),$$

where α_j^i is consumer i's share of supplier j's net income. Thus $\sum_i \alpha_j^i = 1$ for each j. The excess demand $f(p)$ is just

$$\sum_i x^i - \sum_i w^i - \sum_j y^i.$$

Again adding up the budget constraints and rearranging terms yields $p \cdot f(p) \leqslant 0$. This derivation of Walras' law requires only that consumers satisfy their budget constraints, not that they choose optimally or that suppliers maximize net income. Thus the weak form of Walras' law is robust to the behavioral assumptions made about consumers and suppliers. The law remains true even if consumers may borrow from each other, as long as no borrowing from outside the economy takes place. To derive the strong form of Walras' law we need to make assumptions about the behavior of consumers in order to guarantee that they spend all of their income. This will be true, for instance, if they are maximizing a utility function with no local unconstrained maxima.

Theorem 8.3 says that if the domain of f is the closed unit simplex in $\mathbf{R}^{m+1}$ and if f is continuous and satisfies the weak form of Walras' law, then a free disposal equilibrium price vector exists. That is, there is some p for which $f(p) \leqslant 0$. Since only nonnegative prices are considered, if $f(p) \leqslant 0$ and $p \cdot f(p) \leqslant 0$, then whenever $f_i(p) < 0$ it must be that $p_i = 0$. In a free disposal equilibrium a commodity may be excess supply, but then it is free. In order to rule out this possibility it must be that the demand for a commodity must rise faster than supply as its price falls to zero. This means that some restrictions must placed on behavior of the excess demand function as prices tend toward zero. Such a restriction is embodied in the boundary condition (B1) of Theorem 8.5. This boundary condition was introduced by Neuefeind [1980]. It will be satisfied if as the price of commodity i tends toward zero, then the excess demand for commodity i rises indefinitely and the other excess demands do not become too negative. The theorem states that if the excess demand function is defined on the open unit simplex, is continuous and satisfies the strong form of Walras' law and the boundary condition, then an equilibrium price exists. That is, there is some p satisfying $f(p) = 0$.

So far in this analysis, we have restricted prices to belong to the unit simplex. The reason we can do this is that both the budget constraints and the profit functions are positively homogeneous in prices. The budget constraint, $p \cdot x^i \leqslant p \cdot w^i + \sum_j \alpha^i_j(p \cdot y^i)$, defines the same choice set for the consumer if we replace p by λp for any $\lambda \in \mathbf{R}_{++}$. Likewise, maximizing $p \cdot y^i$ or $\lambda p \cdot y^j$ leads to the same choice. Thus we may normalize prices.

The equilibrium price problem has a lot of structure imposed on it from economic considerations. A mathematically more general problem is what is known as the *(nonlinear) complementarity problem.* The function f is no longer assumed to satisfy Walras' law or homogeneity. Instead, f is assumed to be a continuous function whose domain is a closed convex cone C. The problem is to find a p such that $f(p) \in C^*$ and $p \cdot f(p) = 0$. If C is the nonnegative cone $\mathbf{R}^m_+$, then the condition that $f(p) \in C^*$ becomes $f(p) \leqslant 0$. Thus, the major difference between the complementarity problem and the equilibrium price problem is that f is assumed to satisfy Walras' law in the price problem, but it does not have to be defined for the zero price vector. In the complementarity problem f must be defined at zero, but need only satisfy Walras' law at the solution. (The price problem can be extended to cover the case where the excess demand function has a domain determined by a cone other than the nonnegative cone. This is done in Theorem 18.6.) In order to guarantee the existence of a solution to the complementarity problem an additional hypothesis on f is needed. The condition is explicitly given in the statement of Theorem 8.8. Intuitively it limits the size of $p \cdot f(p)$ as p gets large.

The nonlinear complementarity was first studied by Cottle [1966]. The theorem below is due to Karamardian [1971]. The literature on the complementarity problem is extensive. For references to applications see Karamardian [1971] and its references.

In both the price problem and the complementarity problem there is a cone C and function f defined on a subset of C and we are looking for a $p \in C$ satisfying $f(p) \in C^*$. Another way to write this last condition is that $q \cdot f(p) \leqslant 0$ for all $q \in C$. Since in both problems (on the assumption of the strong form of Walras' law), $p \cdot f(p) = 0$, we can rewrite this as $q \cdot f(p) \leqslant p \cdot f(p)$ for all $q \in C$. A system of inequalities of this form is called a system of *variational inequalities* because it compares expressions involving $f(p)$ and p with expressions involving $f(p)$ and q, where q can be viewed as a variation of p. Theorem 8.1 is a result on variational inequalities due to Hartman and Stampacchia [1966].

The intuition involved in these proofs is the following. If a commodity is in excess demand, then its price should be raised and if it is in excess supply, then its price should be lowered. This increases the value of excess of demand. Let us say that price q is better than price p if q gives a higher value to p's excess demand than p does. The variational inequalities tell us that we are looking for a maximal element of this binary relation. Compare this argument to 21.5 below.

8.1 Lemma (Hartman and Stampacchia [1966, Lemma 3.1])
Let $K \subset \mathbf{R}^m$ be compact and convex and let $f : K \to \mathbf{R}^m$ be continuous. Then there exists $\bar{p} \in K$ such that for all $p \in K$,

$$\bar{p} \cdot f(\bar{p}) \geqslant p \cdot f(\bar{p}).$$

Furthermore, the set of such $\bar{p}$ is compact.

8.2 Proof
Define the relation U on K by $q \in U(p)$ if and only if

$$q \cdot f(p) > p \cdot f(p).$$

Since f is continuous, U has open graph. Also $U(p)$ is convex and $p \notin U(p)$ for each $p \in K$. Thus by Fan's lemma (7.5), there is a $\bar{p} \in K$ with $U(\bar{p}) = \varnothing$, i.e., for each $p \in K$ it is not true that $p \cdot f(\bar{p}) > \bar{p} \cdot f(\bar{p})$. Thus for all $p \in K$, $\bar{p} \cdot f(\bar{p}) \geqslant p \cdot f(\bar{p})$. Conversely, any such $\bar{p}$ is U-maximal, so the U-maximal set is compact by 7.5.

8.3 Theorem
Let $f : \Delta_m \to \mathbf{R}^{m+1}$ be continuous and satisfy

$$p \cdot f(p) \leqslant 0 \text{ for all } p.$$

Then the set $\{p \in \Delta : f(p) \leqslant 0\}$ of free disposal equilibrium prices is compact and nonempty.

8.4 Proof
Compactness is immediate. From 8.1 and Walras' law, there is a $\bar{p} \in K$ such that $p \cdot f(\bar{p}) \leqslant \bar{p} \cdot f(\bar{p}) \leqslant 0$ for all $p \in K$. Thus by 2.14(b), $f(\bar{p}) \leqslant 0$.

8.5 Definition
Let $S_m = \{x \in \Delta_m : x_i > 0,\ i = 0,\dots,m+1\}$, the standard m-simplex. The function $f : S \to \mathbf{R}^{m+1}$ satisfies the *boundary condition* (B1) if the following holds.

(B1) there is a $p^* \in S$ and a neighborhood V of $\Delta \setminus S$ in Δ such that for all $p \in V \cap S$, $p^* \cdot f(p) > 0$.

8.6 Theorem (Neuefeind [1980, Lemma 1])
Let $f : S \to \mathbf{R}^{n+1}$ be continuous and satisfy the strong form of Walras' law and the boundary condition (B1):
(SWL) $p \cdot f(p) = 0$.

(B1) there is a $p^* \in S$ and a neighborhood V of $\Delta \setminus S$ in Δ such that for all $p \in V \cap S$, $p^* \cdot f(p) > 0$.
Then the set $\{p : f(p) = 0\}$ of equilibrium prices for f is compact and nonempty.

8.7 Proof (cf. 18.2; Aliprantis and Brown [1982])
Define the binary relation U on Δ by

$$p \in U(q) \text{ if } \begin{cases} p \cdot f(q) > 0 \text{ and } p,q \in S \\ \text{or} \\ p \in S,\, q \in \Delta \setminus S. \end{cases}$$

There are two steps in the proof. The first is to show that the U-maximal elements are precisely the equilibrium prices. The second step is to show that U satisfies the hypotheses of 7.2.

First suppose that $\bar{p}$ is U-maximal, i.e., $U(\bar{p}) = \varnothing$. Since $U(p) = S$ for all $p \in \Delta \setminus S$, we have that $\bar{p} \in S$. Since $\bar{p} \in S$ and $U(\bar{p}) = \varnothing$, we have

$$\text{for each } q \in S,\ q \cdot f(\bar{p}) \leqslant 0.$$

By 2.14(b), $f(\bar{p}) \leqslant 0$. But the strong form of Walras' law says that $\bar{p} \cdot f(\bar{p}) = 0$. Since $\bar{p} \in S$, we must have that $f(\bar{p}) = 0$.

Conversely, if $\bar{p}$ is an equilibrium price, then $0 = f(\bar{p})$ and since $p \cdot 0 = 0$ for all p, $U(\bar{p}) = \varnothing$.

Verify that U satisfies the hypotheses of 7.2:

(ia) $p \notin U(p)$: For $p \in S$ this follows from Walras' law. For $p \in \Delta \setminus S$, $p \notin S = U(p)$.

(ib) $U(p)$ is convex: For $p \in S$, this is immediate. For $p \in \Delta \setminus S$, $U(p) = S$, which is convex.

(ii) If $q \in U^{-1}(p)$, then there is a p' with $q \in \mathit{int}\, U^{-1}(p')$: There are two cases: (a) $q \in S$ and (b) $q \in \Delta \setminus S$.

(iia) $q \in S \cap U^{-1}(p)$. Then $p \cdot f(q) > 0$. Let $H = \{z : p \cdot z > 0\}$. Then by continuity of f, $f^{-1}[H]$ is a neighborhood of q contained in $U^{-1}(p)$.

(iib) $q \in (\Delta \setminus S) \cap U^{-1}(p)$. By boundary condition (B1) $q \in \mathit{int}\, U^{-1}(p^*)$.

8.8 Theorem (Karamardian [1971])
Let C be closed convex cone in $\mathbf{R}^m$ and let $f : C \to \mathbf{R}^m$ be continuous. Suppose that there is a compact convex subset $D \subset C$ satisfying
(i) for every $x \in C \setminus D$ there exists $z \in D$ such that $z \cdot f(x) > x \cdot f(x)$.
Then there exists $\bar{x} \in C$ such that

$$f(\bar{x}) \in C^* \text{ and } \bar{x} \cdot f(\bar{x}) = 0.$$ 8.9

Furthermore, the set of all such $\bar{x}$ is a compact subset of D.

8.10 Proof

Define the binary relation U on C by

$$z \in U(x) \text{ if and only if } z \cdot f(x) > x \cdot f(x).$$

Since C is a closed cone it is σ-compact (7.7). Since f is continuous, U has open graph. The upper contour sets $U(x)$ are convex and don't contain x. Hypothesis (i) implies that if $x \in C \setminus D$, then there is a $z \in D$ with $z \in U(x)$. Thus U satisfies the hypotheses of Proposition 7.8. It follows that the set of U-maximal elements of C is a compact nonempty subset of D. It remains to show that $\bar{x}$ satisfies (8.9) if and only if it is U-maximal.

Suppose $\bar{x}$ is U-maximal. Then for all $z \in C$, $z \cdot f(\bar{x}) \leqslant \bar{x} \cdot f(\bar{x})$. Taking $z = 0$ yields $\bar{x} \cdot f(\bar{x}) \geqslant 0$, and setting $z = 2\bar{x}$ yields $\bar{x} \cdot f(\bar{x}) \leqslant 0$. Thus $\bar{x} \cdot f(\bar{x}) = 0$. Thus for all $z \in C$, $z \cdot f(\bar{x}) \leqslant \bar{x} \cdot f(\bar{x}) = 0$, i.e., $f(\bar{x}) \in C^*$. Thus $\bar{x}$ satisfies (8.9).

Suppose $\bar{x}$ satisfies (8.9). Then since $f(\bar{x}) \in C^*$, for all $z \in C$ it follows that $z \cdot f(\bar{x}) \leqslant 0 = \bar{x} \cdot f(\bar{x})$. Thus $\bar{x}$ is U-maximal.

CHAPTER 9

Some interconnections

9.0 Remark

In this chapter we present a number of alternative proofs of the previous results as well as a few new results. The purpose is to show the interrelatedness of the different techniques developed. For that reason, this chapter may be treated as a selection of exercises with detailed hints. Another reason for presenting many alternative proofs is to present more familiar proofs than those previously presented.

9.1 Brouwer's Theorem (6.6) Implies the K-K-M Lemma (5.4)

Let $K = co\ \{a^i : i = 0,...,m\}$. Then K is convex and compact. Suppose by way of contradiction that $\bigcap_{i=0}^{m} F_i = \varnothing$. Then $\{F_i^c\}$ is an open cover of K and so there is a partition of unity $f_0, \ldots, f_m$ subordinate to it. Define $g : K \to K$ by $g(x) = \sum_{i=0}^{m} f_i(x)a^i$. This g is continuous and hence by 6.6 has a fixed point z. Let $A = \{i : f_i(z) > 0\}$. Then $z \in co\ \{a^i : i \in A\}$ and $z \notin F_i$ for each $i \in A$, which contradicts $co\ \{a^i : i \in A\} \subset \bigcup_{i \in A} F_i$.

9.2 Another Proof of the K-K-M Lemma (5.1) Using Brouwer's Theorem (cf. Peleg [1967])

Let $F_0,...,F_m$ satisfy the hypotheses of 5.1. Set $g_i(x) = dist\ (x,F_i)$ and define $f : \Delta \to \Delta$ by

$$f_i(x) = \frac{x_i + g_i(x)}{1 + \sum_{j=0}^{m} g_j(x)}.$$

The function f is clearly continuous, so by Brouwer's theorem it has a fixed point $\bar{x}$. Now $\bar{x} \in \bigcup_{i=0}^{m} F_i$ by hypothesis, so some $g_i(\bar{x}) = 0$. For this particular i,

$$\bar{x}_i = \frac{\bar{x}_i}{1 + \sum_{j=0}^{m} g_j(\bar{x})},$$

which implies $g_j(\bar{x}) = 0$ for all j. That is, $\bigcap_{j=0}^{m} F_j \neq \emptyset$.

9.3 The K-K-M Lemma (5.1) Implies the Brouwer Theorem (6.1) (K-K-M [1929])

Let $f : \Delta_m \to \Delta_m$ be continuous. Put $F_i = \{z \in \Delta : f_i(z) \leqslant z_i\}$. The collections $\{e^0, \ldots, e^m\}$ and $\{F_0, \ldots, F_m\}$ satisfy the hypotheses of the K-K-M lemma: For suppose $z \in e^{i_0} \cdots e^{i_k}$, then $\sum_{i=0}^{m} f_i(z) = \sum_{j=0}^{k} z_{i_j}$ and therefore at least one $f_{i_j}(z) \leqslant z_{i_j}$, so $z \in F_{i_j}$. Also each F_i is closed as f is continuous. Thus $\bigcap_{i=0}^{m} F_i$ is compact and nonempty but $\bigcap_{i=0}^{m} F_i$ is $\{x \in \Delta : f(x) \leqslant x\}$ which is just the set of fixed points of f.

9.4 The K-K-M Lemma (5.1) Implies the Equilibrium Theorem (8.3) (Gale [1955])

Put $F_i = \{p \in \Delta : f_i(p) \leqslant 0\}$, $i = 0,\ldots,m$. Then $\{e^0, \ldots, e^m\}$ and $\{F_0, \ldots, F_m\}$ satisfy the hypotheses of the K-K-M lemma: For if $p \in co\ \{e^{i_0}, \ldots, e^{i_k}\}$, we cannot have $f_{i_j}(p) > 0$ for all $j = 0,\ldots,k$, since then $p \cdot f(p) = \sum_{j=0}^{k} p_{i_k} f_{i_k}(p) > 0$, a contradiction. Thus $co\ \{e^i : i \in A\} \subset \bigcup_{i \in A} F_i$, for any $A \subset \{0,\ldots,m\}$, and each F_i is closed as f is continuous. Thus $\{p : f(p) \leqslant 0\} = \bigcap_{i=0}^{m} F_i$ is compact and nonempty.

9.5 The Equilibrium Theorem (8.3) Implies the Brouwer Theorem (6.1) (Uzawa [1962])

Let $f : \Delta_m \to \Delta_m$ be continuous. Define $g : \Delta \to \mathbf{R}^{m+1}$ via

$$g(x) = f(x) - \frac{x \cdot f(x)}{x \cdot x}\, x\ .$$

Then g is continuous and satisfies

$$x \cdot g(x) = x \cdot f(x) - \frac{x \cdot f(x)}{x \cdot x}\, x \cdot x = 0 \qquad \text{for all } x,$$

i.e., g projects $f(x)$ onto the hyperplane through zero to which x is normal. Thus by 8.3 there is a $p \in \Delta$ with $g(p) \leqslant 0$, i.e.,

$$f_i(p) \leqslant \frac{p \cdot f(p)}{p \cdot p} p_i \qquad i = 0,\ldots,n. \tag{9.6}$$

If $p_i = 0$ then 9.6, implies $f_i(p) \leqslant 0$ but $f_i(p) \geqslant 0$ as $f(p) \in \Delta$; so $f_i(p) = 0$ and hence

$$f_i(p) = \frac{p \cdot f(p)}{p \cdot p} p_i.$$

If, on the other hand, $p_i > 0$, then $p \cdot g(p) = 0$ and $g(p) \leqslant 0$ imply $g_i(p) = 0$ or

$$f_i(p) = \frac{p \cdot f(p)}{p \cdot p} p_i.$$

Thus 9.6 must hold with equality for each i. Summing then over i yields $\frac{p \cdot f(p)}{p \cdot p} = 1$, so $p = f(p)$.

Thus $g(p) \leqslant 0$ implies $p = f(p)$, and the converse is clearly true. Hence $\{p : g(p) \leqslant 0\} = \{p : p = f(p)\}$.

9.7 Fan's Lemma (7.5) Implies the Equilibrium Theorem (8.3) (Brown [1982])

For each $p \in \Delta$ define $U(p) = \{q \in \Delta : q \cdot f(p) > 0\}$. Then $U(p)$ is convex for each p and Walras' law implies that $p \notin U(p)$. The continuity of f implies that U has open graph. If p is U-maximal, then $U(p) = \varnothing$, so for all $q \in \Delta$, $q \cdot f(p) \leqslant 0$. Thus $f(p) \leqslant 0$. If $f(p) \leqslant 0$, then $q \cdot f(p) \leqslant 0$ for all $q \in \Delta$; so by 7.5, $\{p : f(p) \leqslant 0\}$ is compact and nonempty.

9.8 Fan's Lemma (7.5) Implies Brouwer's Theorem (6.6) (cf. Fan [1969, Theorem 2])

Let $f : K \to K$ be continuous, and for each x set $U(x) = \{y : |y - f(x)| < |x - f(x)|\}$. Then for each x, $U(x)$ is convex, $x \notin U(x)$, and U has open graph. If x is U-maximal, then for all $y \in K$, $|x - f(x)| \leqslant |y - f(x)|$. Picking $y = f(x)$ yields $|x - f(x)| = 0$, so $f(x) = x$. Conversely, if x is a fixed point, then $U(x) = \{y : |y - f(x)| < 0\} = \varnothing$. The conclusion is now immediate from 7.5.

9.9 Remark

The above argument implies the following generalization of Brouwer's fixed point theorem, which in turn yields another proof of Lemma 8.1.

9.10 Proposition (Fan [1969, Theorem 2])

Let $K \subset \mathbf{R}^m$ be nonempty compact and convex, and let $f : K \to \mathbf{R}^m$ be continuous. Then there exists a point $\bar{x} \in K$ such that

$$|\bar{x} - f(\bar{x})| \leqslant |x - f(\bar{x})| \quad \text{for all } x \in K.$$

(Consequently, if $f(K) \subset K$, then $\bar{x}$ is a fixed point of f.)

9.11 Exercise: Proposition 9.10 Implies Lemma 8.1

Hint: Put $g(p) = p + f(p)$, where f satisfies the hypotheses of 8.1. By 9.10 there exists $\bar{p} \in K$ with $|\bar{p} - g(\bar{p})| \leqslant |p - g(\bar{p})|$ for all $p \in K$. Use the argument in 2.10 to conclude that $\bar{p} \cdot f(\bar{p}) \geqslant p \cdot f(\bar{p})$ for all $p \in K$.

9.12 The Brouwer Theorem Implies Theorem 7.2 (cf. Anderson [1977, p. 66])

Suppose $U(x) \neq \varnothing$ for each x. Then for each x there is $y \in U(x)$ and so $x \in U^{-1}(y)$. Thus $\{U^{-1}(y) : y \in K\}$ covers K. By (ii), $\{int\ U^{-1}(y) : y \in K\}$ is an open cover of K. Let $f^1, \ldots, f^k$ be a partition of unity subordinate to the finite subcover $\{int\ U^{-1}(y^1), \ldots, int\ U^{-1}(y^k)\}$. Define the continuous function $g : K \to K$ by $g(x) = \sum_{i=l}^{k} f^i(x)y^i$. It follows from the Brouwer fixed point theorem that g has a fixed point $\bar{x}$. Let $A = \{i : f^i(x) > 0\}$. Then $\bar{x} \in U^{-1}(y^i)$ or $y^i \in U(\bar{x})$ for all $i \in A$. Thus $\bar{x} \in co\ \{y^i : i \in A\} \subset co\ U(\bar{x})$, a contradiction. Thus $\{x : U(x) = \varnothing\}$ is nonempty. It is clearly closed, and hence compact, as K is compact.

9.13 The Brouwer Theorem (6.1) Implies the Equilibrium Theorem (8.3) (cf. 21.5)

Define the price adjustment function $h : \Delta \to \Delta$ by

$$h(p) = \frac{p + f(p)^+}{1 + \sum_i f(p)_i^+}$$

where $f_i(p)^+ = \max\ \{f_i(p),0\}$ and $f(p)^+ = (f_0(p)^+, \ldots, f_n(p)^+)$. This is readily seen to satisfy the hypotheses of 6.1 and so has a fixed point $\bar{p}$, i.e.,

$$\bar{p} = \frac{\bar{p} + f(\bar{p})^+}{1 + \sum_i f_i(\bar{p})^+}.$$

By Walras' law $\bar{p} \cdot f(\bar{p}) \leqslant 0$; so for some i, we must have $\bar{p}_i > 0$ and $f_i(\bar{p}) \leqslant 0$. (Otherwise $\bar{p} \cdot f(\bar{p}) > 0$.) For this i, $f(\bar{p})^+ = 0$, and since

$$\bar{p} = \frac{\bar{p} + f(\bar{p})^+}{1 + \sum_i f_i(\bar{p})^+},$$

it follows that $\sum_i f_i(\bar{p})^+ = 0$. But this implies $f(\bar{p}) \leqslant 0$.

9.14 Lemma 8.1 Implies a Separating Hyperplane Theorem
Let $K_1, K_2 \in \mathbf{R}^m$ be disjoint nonempty compact convex sets. Then there exists a $p \in \mathbf{R}^m$ and $c \in \mathbf{R}$ such that
$\max_{x \varepsilon K_1} p \cdot x < c < \min_{x \varepsilon K_2} p \cdot x.$

9.15 Proof
The set $K = K_2 - K_1$ is compact and convex, and since K_1 and K_2 are disjoint, $0 \notin K$. Define $f : K \to \mathbf{R}^m$ by $f(p) = -p$. Then by 8.1, there exists a $\bar{p} \in K$ such that $\bar{p} \cdot f(\bar{p}) \geqslant p \cdot f(\bar{p})$ for all $p \in K$. Since $0 \notin K$, $0 > (-|\bar{p}|)^2 = \bar{p} \cdot f(\bar{p})$. Thus $\bar{p} \cdot p > 0$ for all $p \in K$, i.e., $\bar{p} \cdot x > \bar{p} \cdot y$ for all $x \in K_2$ and $y \in K_1$. Since K_1 and K_2 are compact, the maximum and minimum values are achieved.

9.16 Exercise: The Brouwer Theorem (6.1) Implies Sperner's Lemma
Prove a weak form of Sperner's lemma, namely that there exists at least one completely labeled subsimplex of a properly labeled subdivision. Hint: Define the mapping $f : \overline{T} \to \overline{T}$ for the vertexes of the subdivision first. If the vertex bears the label i, then f should move it further away from x^i. Then extend f linearly on each subsimplex. If a subsimplex is completely labeled, then all the points move closer to the barycenter, which remains fixed. If the subsimplex is not completely labeled, then all of its points get moved. Thus the only fixed points are barycenters of completely labeled subsimplexes, and by the Brouwer theorem, at least one fixed point exists. (For details see Yoseloff [1974]. Le Van [1982] uses the theory of the topological degree of a mapping to obtain even stronger results.)

9.17 Peleg's Lemma (Peleg [1967])
For each $p \in \Delta_m$ let $U(p)$ be a binary relation on $\{0,...,m\}$, i.e., $U(p)(i) \subset \{0,...,m\}$, $i = 0,...,m$, satisfying

(i) for each $p \in \Delta$, $U(p)$ is acyclic.
(ii) for each $i,j \in \{0,...,m\}$, $\{p \in \Delta : i \in U(p)(j)\}$ is open in Δ.
(iii) $p_j = 0$ implies that j is $U(p)$-maximal.

Then there exists a $\bar{p} \in \Delta$ such that $U(\bar{p}) = \varnothing$, i.e., each $i \in \{0,...,n\}$ is $U(\bar{p})$-maximal.

9.18 Proof
Set $F_i = \{p \in \Delta : \forall j \in \{0,...,m\}, i \notin U(p)(j)\}$. By (ii) each F_i is closed. Suppose $p \in co\ \{e^i : i \in A\}$. Since $U(p)$ is acyclic so is the inverse relation $V(p)$ defined by $i \in V(p)(j)$ if $j \in U(p)(i)$. Since A is finite, it has a $V(p)$-maximal element k. That is for all $j \in A$, $k \notin U(p)(j)$. For $j \notin A$, $p_j = 0$ so $k \notin U(p)(j)$ by (iii). Thus $k \in A$, and for all j, $k \notin U(p)(j)$. Thus $p \in F_k$. Thus the $\{F_i\}$ satisfy the hypotheses of the K-K-M lemma (5.1), so $\bigcap_{i=0}^{m} F_i \neq \varnothing$. For any

$\bar{p} \in \bigcap_{i=0}^{m} F_i$, we have that $i \notin U(p)(j)$ for any i,j.

9.19 Peleg's Lemma (9.17) Implies the K-K-M Lemma (5.1) (Peleg [1967])

Let $\{F_i\}$ be a family of closed sets satisfying (5.2). For each $p \in \Delta$, define

$i \in U(p)(j)$ if and only if $dist\ (p,F_i) > dist\ (p,F_j)$ and $p_j > 0$.

It is easily seen that the $U(p)$ relations satisfy the hypotheses of Peleg's lemma, so there is a $\bar{p} \in \Delta$ satisfying $dist\ (\bar{p},F_i) \leqslant dist\ (\bar{p},F_j)$ for all i,j. Since $\bar{p} \in \bigcup_{i=0}^{n} F_i$ we have that $dist\ (\bar{p},F_k) = 0$ for some k, and so $dist\ (\bar{p},F_i) = 0$ for all i. Thus $\bar{p} \in \bigcap_{i=0}^{m} F_i$.

9.20 Peleg's Lemma (9.17) Implies a Special Case of the Hartman-Stampacchia Lemma (8.1)

Let $f : \Delta \to \mathbf{R}^{m+1}$ be continuous. Define

$i \in U(p)(j)$ if and only if $p_j > 0$ and $f_i(p) > f_j(p)$.

Clearly U satisfies the hypotheses of Peleg's lemma, so there exists a $\bar{p} \in \Delta$ such that $U(p) = \varnothing$. If $\bar{p}_j > 0$, then $f_j(\bar{p}) \geqslant f_i(\bar{p})$ for all i. Let $C = f_j(\bar{p})$ for all j such that $\bar{p}_j > 0$. Then $\bar{p} \cdot f(\bar{p}) = C \geqslant p \cdot f(\bar{p})$ for any $p \in \Delta$.

9.21 Remark

The use of Theorem 7.2 as a tool for proving other theorems is closely related to the work of Dugundji and Granas [1978; 1982] and Granas [1981]. They call a correspondence $G : X \twoheadrightarrow \mathbf{R}^m$ a *K-K-M map* if $co\ \{x_1,...,x_n\} \subset \bigcup_{i=1}^{n} G(x_i)$ for every finite subset $\{x_1,...,x_n\} \subset X$. By Fan's generalization of the K-K-M lemma (5.7), if G is a compact-valued K-K-M map, then $\bigcap_{x \in X} G(x) \neq \varnothing$. Let U be a binary relation on a compact convex set K satisfying the hypotheses of 7.2. Then G defined by $G(x) = K \setminus int\ U(x)$ is a K-K-M map. (This is how Theorem 7.2 was proven.) Thus all of the arguments that we make using Theorem 7.2 have a dual argument based on K-K-M maps. As a practical matter, the hypotheses of 7.2 seem easier to verify than the property of being a K-K-M map. Also the notion of maximization as a tool for proving existence has a lot of intuitive appeal.

CHAPTER 10

What good is a completely labeled subsimplex

10.0 Remark

The proof of Sperner's lemma given in 4.3 suggests an algorithm for finding completely labeled subsimplexes. Cohen [1967] uses the following argument for proving Sperner's lemma. The suggestive terminology is borrowed from a lecture by David Schmeidler. Consider the simplex to be a house and all the n-subsimplexes to be rooms. The completely labeled $(n-1)$-subsimplexes are doors. A completely labeled n-simplex is a room with only one door. The induction hypothesis asserts that there are an odd number of doors to the outside. If we enter one of these doors and keep going from room to room we either end up in a room with only one door or back outside. If we end up in a room with only one door, we have found a completely labeled subsimplex. If we come back outside there are still an odd number of doors to the outside that we have not yet used. Thus an odd number of them must lead to a room inside with only one door.

The details involved in implementing a computational procedure based on this "path-following" approach are beyond the scope of these notes. An excellent reference for this subject is Scarf [1973] or Todd [1976]. In this chapter we will see that finding completely labeled subsimplexes allows us to approximate fixed points of functions, maximal elements of binary relations, and intersections of sets.

10.1 Remark: Completely Labeled Subsimplexes and the K-K-M Lemma

Section 5.3 presents a proof of the K-K-M lemma based on simplicial subdivision and Sperner's lemma. In 5.3 a point in $\bigcap F_i$ is found as the limit of the vertexes of a sequence of completely labeled subsimplexes. This suggests that a small enough completely labeled subsimplex ought to be close to $\bigcap F_i$. The next theorem makes this notion more precise.

10.2 Theorem

Let $\{F_0,...,F_m\}$ satisfy the hypotheses of the K-K-M lemma (5.1). Let Δ be simplicially subdivided and labeled as in 5.3. Set $F = \bigcap_{i=0}^{m} F_i$. Then for every $\varepsilon > 0$ there is a $\delta > 0$, such that if the mesh of the subdivision is less than δ, then every completely labeled subsimplex lies in $N_\varepsilon(F)$.

10.3 Proof

Put $g^i(x) = dist\ (x,F_i)$ and $g = \max_i g^i$. Since $K \setminus (N_\varepsilon(F))$ is compact, and g is continuous (2.7) it follows that g achieves a minimum value $\delta > 0$. Let $x^0 \cdots x^m$ be a completely labeled subsimplex of diameter $< \delta$ containing the point x. Since $x^0 \cdots x^m$ is completely labeled, $x^i \in F_i$ and so $dist\ (x,F_i) \leqslant |x - x_i| < \delta$ for all i. Thus $g(x) < \delta$, so $x \in N_\varepsilon(F)$.

10.4 Remark: Approximating Fixed Points

Theorem 10.2 yields a similar result for the set of fixed points of a function. Section 9.4 presents a proof of the Brouwer fixed point theorem based on the K-K-M lemma. This argument and 10.2 provide the proof of the following theorem (10.5). A related line of reasoning provides a proof of the notion that if a point doesn't move too much it must be near a fixed point. This is the gist of Theorem 10.7.

10.5 Theorem

Let $f : \Delta \rightarrow \Delta$ and put $F = \{z : f(z) = z\}$. Let Δ be subdivided and labeled as in 6.2. Then for every $\varepsilon > 0$ there is a $\delta > 0$, such that if the mesh of the subdivision is less than δ, then every completely labeled subsimplex lies in $N_\varepsilon(F)$.

10.6 Proof (cf. 9.3)

Put $F_i = \{z : f_i(z) \leqslant z_i\}$. Then each F_i is closed and $F = \bigcap_{i=0}^{m} F_i$. If the simplex $x^0...x^m$ is completely labeled, then $x^i \in F_i$ and the conclusion follows from 10.2.

10.7 Theorem

Let f satisfy the hypotheses of Brouwer's fixed point theorem (6.6) and let F be the set of fixed points of f. Then for every $\varepsilon > 0$ there is a $\delta > 0$ such that $|f(z) - z| < \delta$ implies $z \in N_\varepsilon(F)$.

10.8 Proof (Green [1981])

Set $g(z) = |f(z) - z|$. Since $C = K \setminus N_\varepsilon(F)$ is compact and g is continuous, $\delta = \min_{z \varepsilon C} g(z)$ satisfies the conclusion of the theorem.

10.9 Remark: Approximating Maximal Elements

The set of maximal elements of a binary relation U on K is $\bigcap_{z \in K} (K \setminus U^{-1}(z))$. If U has open graph, then we may approximate this intersection by a finite intersection. This is proven in Theorem 10.11.

10.10 Definition

A set D is δ-*dense* in K if every open set of diameter δ meets D. It follows that if K is compact, then for every $\delta > 0$, K has a finite δ-dense subset.

10.11 Theorem

Let K be compact and let U be a binary relation on K with open graph. Let M be the set of maximal elements of U. For every $\varepsilon > 0$, there is a $\delta > 0$ such that if D is δ-dense in K, then
$\bigcap_{z \in D} K \setminus U^{-1}(z) \subset N_\varepsilon(M)$.

10.12 Proof

Let $x \in K \setminus M$. Then there is a $y_x \in U(x)$, and since U has open graph, there is a δ_x such that $N_{\delta_x}(x) \times N_{\delta_x}(y_x) \subset Gr\ U$. Since $C = K \setminus N_\varepsilon(M)$ is compact, it is covered by a finite collection $\{N_{\delta_i}(x_i)\}$. Put $\delta = \min_i \delta_i$.

Let $x \notin N_\varepsilon(M)$. Then $x \in C$ and so $x \in N_{\delta_i}(x_i)$ for some i. Since D is δ-dense, let $z \in D \cap N_{\delta_i}(y_i)$. Since $N_{\delta_i}(x_i) \times N_{\delta_i}(y_i) \subset Gr\ U$, we have that $x \in U^{-1}(z)$ and so $x \notin K \setminus U^{-1}(z)$.

Thus $\bigcap_{z \in D} K \setminus U^{-1}(z) \subset N_\varepsilon(M)$.

CHAPTER 11

Continuity of correspondences

11.0 Remark

A correspondence is a function whose values are sets of points. Notions of continuity for correspondences can traced back to Kuratowski [1932] and Bouligand [1932]. Berge [1959, Ch. 6] and Hildenbrand [1974, Ch. B] have collected most of the relevant theorems on continuity of correspondences. It is difficult to attribute most of these theorems, but virtually all of the results of this chapter can be found in Berge [1959]. Whenever possible, citations are provided for theorems not found there. Due to slight differences in terminology, the proofs presented here are generally not identical to those of Berge. A particular difference in terminology is that Berge requires compact-valuedness as part of the definition of upper semi-continuity. Since these properties seem to be quite distinct, that requirement is not made here. In applications, it frequently makes no difference, as the correspondences under consideration have compact values anyway. Moore [1968] has catalogued a number of differences between different possible definitions of semi-continuity. The term hemi-continuity has now replaced semi-continuity in referring to correspondences. It helps to avoid confusion with semi-continuity of real-valued functions.

The chief use of correspondences in economic and game theoretic problems is the linking up of multi-player situations and single-player situations. For example, the problem of finding a maximal element of a binary relation as discussed in Chapter 7 is a single-player problem. The solution to the problem does not depend on the actions of others. As another example, the problem of finding an equilibrium price vector can be reduced to a single-player maximization problem as is shown in Chapter 8. The problem of finding a noncooperative equilibrium of a multi-player game is on the face of it of a different sort. It amounts to solving several interdependent individual maximization problems simultaneously. Given a choice of variables for all but one of the maximization problems we can find the set of solutions for the remaining problem. This solution will in general depend on the choices of the other players and so defines a correspondence mapping the set of joint choice variables into itself. A noncooperative equilibrium will be a fixed point of this correspondence. Theorems on the existence of fixed points for correspondences are presented in Chapter 15. There are of course other uses for correspondences, even in single-player problems such as the equilibrium price problem, as is shown in Chapter 18. On the other hand, it is also possible to reduce multi-player situations to situations involving a single fictitious player, as in 19.7.

The general method of proof for results about correspondences is to reduce the problem to one involving (single-valued) functions. The single-valued function will either approximate the correspondence or be a selection from it. The theorems of Chapters 13 and 14 are all in this vein. In a sense these techniques eliminate the need for any othe theorems about correspondences, since they can be proved by using only theorems about functions. Thus it is always possible to substitute the use of Brouwer's fixed point theorem for the use of Kakutani's fixed point theorem, for example. While Brouwer's theorem is marginally easier to prove, it is frequently the case that it is more intuitive to define a correspondence than to construct an approximating function.

11.1 Definition

Let 2^Y denote the power set of Y, i.e., the collection of all subsets of Y. A *correspondence* (or *multivalent function*) γ from X to Y is a function from X to the family of subsets of Y. We denote this by $\gamma : X \twoheadrightarrow Y$. (Binary relations as defined in 7.1 can be viewed as correspondences from a set into itself.) For a correspondence $\gamma : E \twoheadrightarrow F$, let $Gr\ \gamma$ denote the *graph* of γ, i.e.,

$$Gr\ \gamma = \{(x,y) \in E \times F : y \in \gamma(x)\}.$$

Likewise, for a function $f : E \to F$

$$Gr\ f = \{(x,y) \in E \times F : y = f(x)\}.$$

11.2 Definition

Let $\gamma : X \twoheadrightarrow Y$, $E \subset Y$ and $F \subset X$. The *image* of F under γ is defined by

$$\gamma(F) = \bigcup_{x \in F} \gamma(x).$$

The *upper* (or *strong*) *inverse* of E under γ, denoted $\gamma^+[E]$, is defined by

$$\gamma^+[E] = \{x \in X : \gamma(x) \subset E\}.$$

The *lower* (or *weak*) *inverse* of E under γ, denoted $\gamma^{-}[E]$, is defined by

$$\gamma^{-}[E] = \{x \in X : \gamma(x) \cap E \neq \emptyset\}.$$

For $y \in Y$, set

$$\gamma^{-1}(y) = \{x \in X : y \in \gamma(x)\}.$$

Note that $\gamma^{-1}(y) = \gamma^{-}[\{y\}]$. (If U is a binary relation on X, i.e., $U : X \twoheadrightarrow X$, then this definition is consistent with the definition of $U^{-1}(y)$ in 7.1.)

11.3 Definition

A correspondence $\gamma : X \twoheadrightarrow Y$ is called *upper hemi-continuous (uhc) at* x if whenever x is in the upper inverse of an open set so is a neighborhood of x; and γ is *lower hemi-continuous (lhc) at* x if whenever x is in the lower inverse of an open set so is a neighborhood of x. The correspondence $\gamma : X \twoheadrightarrow Y$ is *upper hemi-continuous* (resp. *lower hemi-continuous*) if it is upper hemi-continuous (resp. lower hemi-continuous) at every $x \in X$. Thus γ is upper hemi-continuous (resp. lower hemi-continuous) if the upper (resp. lower) inverses of open sets are open. A correspondence is called *continuous* if it is both upper and lower hemi-continuous.

11.4 Note

If $\gamma : X \twoheadrightarrow Y$ is singleton-valued it can be considered as a function from X to Y and we may sometimes identify the two. In this case the upper and lower inverses of a set coincide and agree with the inverse regarded as a function. Either form of hemi-continuity is equivalent to continuity as a function. The term "semi-continuity" has been used to mean hemi-continuity, but this usage can lead to confusion when discussing real-valued singleton correspondences. A semi-continuous real-valued function (2.27) is not a hemi-continuous correspondence unless it is also continuous.

11.5 Definition

The correspondence $\gamma : E \twoheadrightarrow F$ is said to be *closed at* x if whenever $x^n \to x$, $y^n \in \gamma(x^n)$ and $y^n \to y$, then $y \in \gamma(x)$. A correspondence is said to be *closed* if it is closed at every point of its domain, i.e., if its graph is closed. The correspondence γ is said to be *open* or have *open graph* if $Gr\ \gamma$ is open in $E \times F$.

11.6 Definition

A correspondence $\gamma : E \twoheadrightarrow F$ is said to have *open* (resp. *closed*) *sections* if for each $x \in E$, $\gamma(x)$ is open (resp. closed) in F, and for each $y \in F$, $\gamma^{-}[\{y\}]$ is open (resp. closed) in E.

11.7 Note

There has been some blurring in the literature of the distinction between closed correspondences and upper hemi-continuous correspondences. The relationship between the two notions is set forth in 11.8 and 11.9 below. For closed-valued correspondences into a compact space the two definitions coincide and the distinction may seem pedantic. Nevertheless the distinction is important in some circumstances. (See, for example, 11.23 below or Moore [1968].)

11.8 Examples: Closedness vs. Upper Hemi-continuity

In general, a correspondence may be closed without being upper hemi-continuous, and vice versa.

Define $\gamma : \mathbf{R} \twoheadrightarrow \mathbf{R}$ via

$$\gamma(x) = \begin{cases} \{1/x\} & \text{for } x \neq 0 \\ \{0\} & \text{for } x = 0 \end{cases}$$

Then γ is closed but not upper hemi-continuous.

Define $\mu : \mathbf{R} \twoheadrightarrow \mathbf{R}$ via $\mu(x) = (0,1)$. Then μ is upper hemi-continuous but not closed.

11.9 Proposition: Closedness, Openness and Hemi-continuity

Let $E \subset \mathbf{R}^m$, $F \subset \mathbf{R}^k$ and let $\gamma : E \twoheadrightarrow F$.

(a) If γ is upper hemi-continuous and closed-valued, then γ is closed.

(b) If F is compact and γ is closed, then γ is upper hemi-continuous.

(c) If γ is open, then γ is lower hemi-continuous.

(d) If γ is singleton-valued at x and upper hemi-continuous at x, then γ is continuous at x.

(e) If γ has open lower sections, then γ is lower hemi-continuous.

11.10 Proof

(a) Suppose $(x,y) \notin Gr\,\gamma$. Then since γ is closed-valued, there is a closed neighborhood U of y disjoint from $\gamma(x)$. Then $V = U^c$ is an open neighborhood of $\gamma(x)$. Since γ is upper hemi-continuous, $\gamma^+[V]$ contains an open neighborhood W of x, i.e., $\gamma(z) \subset V$ for all $z \in W$. Thus $(W \times U) \cap Gr\,\gamma = \varnothing$ and $(x,y) \in W \times U$. Hence the complement of $Gr\,\gamma$ is open, so $Gr\,\gamma$ is closed.

(b) Suppose not. Then there is some x and an open neighborhood U of $\gamma(x)$ such that for every neighborhood V of x, there is a $z \in V$ with $\gamma(z) \not\subset U$. Thus we can find $z^n \to x$, $y^n \in \gamma(z^n)$ with $y^n \notin U$. Since F is compact, $\{y^n\}$ has a convergent subsequence converging to $y \notin U$. But since γ is closed, $(x,y) \in Gr\ \gamma$, so $y \in \gamma(x) \subset U$, a contradiction.

(c) Exercise.

(d) Exercise.

(e) Exercise.

11.11 Proposition: Sequential Characterizations of Hemi-continuity
Let $E \subset \mathbf{R}^m$, $F \subset \mathbf{R}^k$, $\gamma : E \twoheadrightarrow F$.

(a) If γ is compact-valued, then γ is upper hemi-continuous at x if and only if for every sequence $x^n \to x$ and $y^n \in \gamma(x^n)$ there is a convergent subsequence of $\{y^n\}$ with limit in $\gamma(x)$.

(b) Then γ is lower hemi-continuous if and only if $x^n \to x$ and $y \in \gamma(x)$ imply that there is a sequence $y^n \in \gamma(x^n)$ with $y^n \to y$.

11.12 Proof

(a) Suppose γ is upper hemi-continuous at x, $x^n \to x$ and $y^n \in \gamma(x^n)$. Since γ is compact-valued, $\gamma(x)$ has a bounded neighborhood U. Since γ is upper hemi-continuous, there is a neighborhood V of x such that $\gamma(V) \subset U$. Thus $\{y^n\}$ is eventually in U, thus bounded, and so has a convergent subsequence. Since compact sets are closed, this limit belongs to $\gamma(x)$.

Now suppose that for every sequence $x^n \to x$, $y^n \in \gamma(x^n)$, there is a subsequence of $\{y^n\}$ with limit in $\gamma(x)$. Suppose γ is not upper hemi-continuous; then there is a neighborhood U of x and a sequence $z^n \to x$ with $y^n \in \gamma(z^n)$ and $y^n \notin U$. Such a sequence $\{y^n\}$ can have no subsequence with limit in $\gamma(x)$, a contradiction.

(b) Exercise.

11.13 Definition
A convex set F is a *polytope* if it is the convex hull of a finite set. In particular, a simplex is a polytope.

11.14 Proposition: Open Sections vs. Open Graph (cf. Shafer [1974], Bergstrom, Parks, and Rader [1976])
Let $E \subset \mathbf{R}^m$ and $F \subset \mathbf{R}^k$ and let F be a polytope. If $\gamma : E \twoheadrightarrow F$ is convex-valued and has open sections, then γ has open graph.

11.15 Proof
Let $y \in \gamma(x)$. Since γ has open sections and F is a polytope, there is a polytope neighborhood U of y contained in $\gamma(x)$. Let $U = co\ \{y^1,\ldots,y^n\}$. Since γ has open sections, for each i there is a neighborhood of x, V_i, such that $y^i \in \gamma(z)$ for all $z \in V_i$. Put

$V = \bigcap_{i=1}^{n} V_i$ and $W = V \times U$ and let $(x',y') \in W$. Then $y^i \in \gamma(x')$, $i = 1,\ldots,n$ and $y' \in U = co\ \{y^1,\ldots,y^n\} \subset co\ \gamma(x')$, since γ is convex-valued. Thus W is a neighborhood of (x,y) completely contained in $Gr\ \gamma$.

11.16 Proposition: Upper Hemi-continuous Image of a Compact Set
Let $\gamma : E \twoheadrightarrow F$ be upper hemi-continuous and compact-valued and let $K \subset E$ be compact. Then $\gamma(K)$ is compact.

11.17 Proof (Berge [1959])
Let $\{U_\alpha\}$ be an open covering of $\gamma(K)$. Since $\gamma(x)$ is compact, there is a finite subcover $U_{x^1},\ldots,U_{x^{n_x}}$, of $\gamma(x)$. Put $V_x = U_x^1 \cup , \ldots , \cup U_{x^{n_x}}$. Then since γ is upper hemi-continuous, $\gamma^+[V_x]$ is open and contains x. Hence K is covered by a finite number of $\gamma^+[V_x]$'s and the corresponding U_x^i's are a finite cover of $\gamma(K)$.

11.18 Exercise: Miscellaneous Facts about Hemi-continuous Correspondences
Let $E \subset \mathbf{R}^m$.

(a) Let $\gamma : E \twoheadrightarrow \mathbf{R}^m$ be upper hemi-continuous with closed values. Then the set of fixed points of γ, i.e., $\{x \in E : x \in \gamma(x)\}$, is a closed (possibly empty) subset of E.

(b) Let $\gamma,\mu : E \twoheadrightarrow \mathbf{R}^m$ be upper hemi-continuous with closed values. Then $\{x \in E : \mu(x) \cap \gamma(x) \neq \emptyset\}$ is a closed (possibly empty) subset of E.

(c) Let $\gamma : E \twoheadrightarrow \mathbf{R}^m$ be lower hemi-continuous. Then $\{x \in E : \gamma(x) \neq \emptyset\}$ is an open subset of E.

(d) Let $\gamma : E \twoheadrightarrow \mathbf{R}^m$ be upper hemi-continuous. Then $\{x \in E : \gamma(x) \neq \emptyset\}$ is a closed subset of E.

(e) Let $X \subset \mathbf{R}^m$ be closed, convex, and bounded below and let $\beta : \mathbf{R}_+^{m+1} \twoheadrightarrow X$ be defined by $\beta(p,M) = \{x \in X : p \cdot x \leqslant M\}$, where $M \in \mathbf{R}_+$ and $p \in \mathbf{R}_+^m$. In other words, β is a budget correspondence for the consumption set X. Show that β is upper hemi-continuous; and if there is some $x \in X$ satisfying $p \cdot x < M$, then β is lower hemi-continuous at (p,M).

11.19 Proposition: Closure of a Correspondence
Let $E \subset \mathbf{R}^m$ and $F \subset \mathbf{R}^k$

(a) Let $\gamma : E \twoheadrightarrow F$ be upper hemi-continuous at x. Then $\bar{\gamma} : E \twoheadrightarrow F$, defined by

$$\bar{\gamma}(x) = \textit{closure (in F) of } \gamma(x)$$

is upper hemi-continuous at x.

(b) The converse of (a) is not true.

(c) The correspondence $\gamma : E \twoheadrightarrow F$ is lower hemi-continuous at x if and only if $\overline{\gamma} : E \twoheadrightarrow F$ is lower hemi-continuous at x.

11.20 Proof

Exercise. Hints:

(a) Use the fact that if E and F are disjoint closed sets in $\mathbf{R}^m$, then they have disjoint open neighborhoods.

(b) Consider $\gamma : \mathbf{R} \twoheadrightarrow \mathbf{R}$ via $\gamma(x) = \{x\}^c$.

(c) Use the Cantor diagonal process and 11.11.

11.21 Proposition: Intersections of Correspondences

Let $E \subset \mathbf{R}^m$, $F \subset \mathbf{R}^k$ and $\gamma,\mu : E \twoheadrightarrow F$, and define $(\gamma \cap \mu) : E \twoheadrightarrow F$ by $(\gamma \cap \mu)(x) = \gamma(x) \cap \mu(x)$. Suppose $\gamma(x) \cap \mu(x) \neq \varnothing$.

(a) If γ and μ are upper hemi-continuous at x and closed-valued, then $(\gamma \cap \mu)$ is upper hemi-continuous at x. (Hildenbrand [1974, Prop. 2a., p. 23].)

(b) If μ is closed at x and γ is upper hemi-continuous at x and $\gamma(x)$ is compact then $(\gamma \cap \mu)$ is upper hemi-continuous at x. (Berge [1959, Th. 7, p. 117].)

(c) If γ is lower hemi-continuous at x and if μ has open graph, then $(\gamma \cap \mu)$ is lower hemi-continuous at x. (Prabhakar and Yannelis [1983, Lemma 3.2].)

11.22 Proof

Let U be an open neighborhood of $\gamma(x) \cap \mu(x)$. Put $C = \gamma(x) \cap U^c$.

(a) Note that C is closed and $\mu(x) \cap C = \varnothing$. Thus there are disjoint open sets V_1 and V_2 with $\mu(x) \subset V_1$, $C \subset V_2$. Since μ is upper hemi-continuous at x, there is a neighborhood W_1 of x with $\mu(W_1) \subset V_1 \subset V_2^c$. Now $\gamma(x) \subset U \cup V_2$, which is open and so x has a neighborhood W_2 with $\gamma(W_2) \subset U \cup V_2$, as γ is upper hemi-continuous at x. Put $W = W_1 \cap W_2$. Then for $z \in W$, $\gamma(z) \cap \mu(z) \subset V_2^c \cap (U \cup V_2) \subset U$. Thus $(\gamma \cap \mu)$ is upper hemi-continuous at x.

(b) Note that in this case C is compact and $\mu(x) \cap C = \varnothing$. Since μ is closed at x, if $y \notin \mu(x)$ then we cannot have $y^n \to y$, where $y^n \in \mu(x^n)$ and $x^n \to x$. Thus there is a neighborhood U_y of y and W_y of x with $\mu(W_y) \subset U_y^c$. Since C is compact, we can write $C \subset V_2 = U_{y^1} \cup \cdots \cup U_{y^n}$; so setting $W_1 = W_{y^1} \cap \cdots \cap W_{y^n}$, we have $\mu(W_1) \subset V_2^c$. The rest of the proof is as in (a).

(c) Let U be open and let $y \in (\gamma \cap \mu)(x) \cap U$. Since μ has open graph, there is a neighborhood $W \times V$ of (x,y)

contained in $Gr\ \mu$. Since γ is lower hemi-continuous, $\gamma^{-}[U \cap V] \cap W$ is a neighborhood of x, and if $z \in \gamma^{-}[U \cap V] \cap W$, then $y \in (\gamma \cap \mu)(z) \cap U$. Thus $(\gamma \cap \mu)$ is lower hemi-continuous.

11.23 Proposition: Composition of Correspondences
Let $\mu : E \twoheadrightarrow F$, $\gamma : F \twoheadrightarrow G$. Define $\gamma \circ \mu : E \twoheadrightarrow G$ via $\gamma \circ \mu(x) = \bigcup_{y \in \mu(x)} \gamma(y)$.

(a) If γ and μ are upper hemi-continuous, so is $\gamma \circ \mu$.
(b) If γ and μ are lower hemi-continuous, so is $\gamma \circ \mu$.
(c) If γ and μ are closed, $\gamma \circ \mu$ may fail to be closed.

11.24 Proof
Exercise. Hint for (c) (Moore [1968]): Let $E = \{\alpha \in \mathbf{R} : -\frac{\pi}{4} \leqslant \alpha \leqslant \frac{\pi}{4}\}$, $F = \{(x_1,x_2) \in \mathbf{R}^2 : x_1 \geqslant 0\}$ and $G = \mathbf{R}$. Set $\mu(\alpha) = \{(x_1,x_2) \in F : |x_2| \leqslant |x_1 \tan \alpha|; \alpha x_2 \geqslant 0\}$, i.e., $\mu(\alpha)$ is the set of points in F lying between the x_1-axis and a ray making angle α with the axis. Set $\gamma((x_1,x_2)) = \{x_2\}$.

11.25 Proposition: Products of Correspondences
Let $\gamma_i : E \twoheadrightarrow F_i$, $i = 1,\dots,k$.

(a) If each γ_i is upper hemi-continuous at x and compact-valued, then

$$\prod_i \gamma_i : z \mapsto \prod_i \gamma_i(z)$$

is upper hemi-continuous at x and compact-valued.
(b) If each γ_i is lower hemi-continuous at x, then $\prod_i \gamma_i$ is lower hemi-continuous at x.
(c) If each γ_i is closed at x, then $\prod_i \gamma_i$ is closed at x.
(d) If each γ_i has open graph, then $\prod_i \gamma_i$ has open graph.

11.26 Proof
Exercise. Assertion (a) follows from 11.11(a), (b) from 11.11(b) and (c) and (d) from the definitions.

11.27 Proposition: Sums of Correspondences
Let $\gamma_i : E \twoheadrightarrow F_i$, $i = 1,\dots,k$.

(a) If each γ_i is upper hemi-continuous at x and compact-valued, then

$$\sum_i \gamma_i : z \mapsto \sum_i \gamma_i(z)$$

is upper hemi-continuous at x and compact-valued.

(b) If each γ_i is lower hemi-continuous at x, then $\sum_i \gamma_i$ is lower hemi-continuous at x.

(c) If each γ_i has open graph, then $\sum_i \gamma_i$ has open graph.

11.28 Proof

Exercise. Assertion (a) follows from 2.43 and 11.11(a), (b) from 11.11(b), and (c) from the definitions.

11.29 Proposition: Convex Hull of a Correspondence

Let $\gamma : E \twoheadrightarrow F$, where F is convex.

(a) If γ is compact-valued and upper hemi-continuous at x, then

$$co\ \gamma : z \mapsto co\ \gamma(z)$$

is upper hemi-continuous at x.

(b) If γ is lower hemi-continuous at x, $co\ \gamma$ is lower hemi-continuous at x.

(c) If γ has open graph, then $co\ \gamma$ has open graph.

(d) Even if γ is a compact-valued closed correspondence, $co\ \gamma$ may still fail to be closed.

11.30 Proof

The proof is left as an exercise. For parts (a) and (b) use Caratheodory's theorem (2.3) and 11.9(c) and 11.11. For part (d) consider the correspondence $\gamma : \mathbf{R} \twoheadrightarrow \mathbf{R}$ via

$$\gamma(x) = \begin{cases} \{0, 1/x\} & x \neq 0 \\ \{0\} & x = 0. \end{cases}$$

11.31 Proposition: Open Sections vs. Open Graph Revisited

Let $E \subset \mathbf{R}^m$ and $F \subset \mathbf{R}^k$ and let F be a polytope. If $\gamma : E \twoheadrightarrow F$ has open sections, then $co\ \gamma$ has open graph.

11.32 Proof

By 11.14, we need only show that $co\ \gamma$ has open sections. Since $\gamma(x)$ is open for each x, so is $co\ \gamma(x)$. (Exercise 2.5c.) Next let $x \in (co\ \gamma)^{-}[\{y\}]$, i.e., $y \in co\ \gamma(x)$. We wish to find a neighborhood U of x such that $w \in U$ implies $y \in co\ \gamma(w)$. Since $y \in co\ \gamma(x)$, we can write $y = \sum_{i=1}^{n} \lambda_i z_i$, where each $z_i \in \gamma(x)$ and the λ_i's are nonnegative and sum to unity. Since γ has open sections, for each i there is a neighborhood U_i of x in $\gamma^{-}[\{z_i\}]$. Setting $U = \bigcap_{i=1}^{n} U_i$, we have that $w \in U$ implies $z_i \in \gamma(w)$ for all i, so that $y \in co\ \{z_1,\ldots,z_n\} \subset co\ \gamma(w)$. Thus $co\ \gamma$ has open sections.

11.33 Note

It follows from 11.29(d) that the analogue of Proposition 11.31 for correspondences with closed sections is false.

CHAPTER 12

The maximum theorem

12.0 Remarks

One of the most useful and powerful theorems employed in mathematical economics and game theory is the "maximum theorem." It states that the set of solutions to a maximization problem varies upper hemi-continuously as the constraint set of the problem varies in a continuous way. Theorem 12.1 is due to Berge [1959] and considers the case of maximizing a continuous real-valued function over a compact set which varies continuously with some parameter vector. The set of solutions is an upper hemi-continuous correspondence with compact values. Furthermore, the value of the maximized function varies continuously with the parameters. Theorem 12.3 is due to Walker [1979] and extends Berge's theorem to the case of maximal elements of an open binary relation. Theorem 12.3 allows the binary relation as well as the constraint set to vary with the parameters. Similar results may be found in Sonnenschein [1971] and Debreu [1969]. Theorem 12.5 weakens the requirement of open graph to the requirement that the nonmaximal set be open, at the expense of requiring the constraint set to fixed and independent of the parameters. The remaining theorems are applications of the principles to problems encountered in later chapters.

In the statement of the theorems, the set G should be interpreted as the set of parameters, and Y or X as the set of alternatives. For instance, in 11.8(e) it is shown that the budget correspondence, $\beta : (p,m) \mapsto\!\!\!\rightarrow \{x \in \mathbf{R}^m_+ : p \cdot x \leqslant m, x \geqslant 0\}$ is continuous for $m > 0$ and compact-valued for $p > 0$. The set of parameters is then $G = \mathbf{R}^m_{++} \times \mathbf{R}_{++}$, the set of price-income pairs. If a consumer has a preference relation satisfying the hypotheses of 7.5, then Theorem 12.3 says that his demand correspondence is upper hemi-continuous. Likewise, supply correspondences are upper hemi-continuous, so that excess demand correspondences are upper hemi-continuous, provided consumers have strictly positive income.

12.1 Theorem (Berge [1959])
Let $G \subset \mathbf{R}^m$, $Y \subset \mathbf{R}^k$ and let $\gamma : G \twoheadrightarrow Y$ be a compact-valued correspondence. Let $f : Y \to \mathbf{R}$ be continuous. Define $\mu : G \twoheadrightarrow Y$ by $\mu(x) = \{y \in \gamma(x) : y \text{ maximizes } f \text{ on } \gamma(x)\}$, and $F : G \to \mathbf{R}$ by $F(x) = f(y)$ for $y \in \mu(x)$. If γ is continuous at x, then μ is closed and upper hemi-continuous at x and F is continuous at x. Furthermore, μ is compact-valued.

12.2 Proof
First note that since γ is compact-valued, μ is nonempty and compact-valued. It suffices to show that μ is closed at x, for then $\mu = \gamma \cap \mu$ and 11.21(b) implies that μ is upper hemi-continuous at x. Let $x^n \to x$, $y^n \in \mu(x^n)$, $y^n \to y$. We wish to show $y \in \mu(x)$ and $F(x^n) \to F(x)$. Since γ is upper hemi-continuous and compact-valued, 11.9(a) implies that indeed $y \in \gamma(x)$. Suppose $y \notin \mu(x)$. Then there is $z \in \gamma(x)$ with $f(z) > f(y)$. Since γ is lower hemi-continuous at x, by 11.11 there is a sequence $z^n \to z$, $z^n \in \gamma(x^n)$. Since $z^n \to z$, $y^n \to y$ and $f(z) > f(y)$, the continuity of f implies that eventually $f(z^n) > f(y^n)$, contradicting $y^n \in \mu(x^n)$. Now $F(x^n) = f(y^n) \to f(y) = F(x)$, so F is continuous at x.

12.3 Theorem (Walker [1979], cf. Sonnenschein [1971])
Let $G \subset \mathbf{R}^m$, $Y \subset \mathbf{R}^k$, and let $\gamma : G \twoheadrightarrow Y$ be upper hemi-continuous with compact values. Let $U : Y \times G \twoheadrightarrow Y$ have an open graph. Define $\mu : G \twoheadrightarrow Y$ by $\mu(x) = \{y \in \gamma(x) : U(y,x) \cap \gamma(x) = \varnothing\}$. If γ is closed and lower hemi-continuous at x, then μ is closed at x. If in addition, γ is upper hemi-continuous at x, then μ is upper hemi-continuous at x. Further, μ has compact (but possibly empty) values.

12.4 Proof
Since U has open graph, $\mu(x)$ is closed (its complement being clearly open) in $\gamma(x)$, which is compact. Thus μ has compact values.

Let $x^n \to x$, $y^n \in \mu(x^n)$, $y^n \to y$. We wish to show that $y \in \mu(x)$. Since γ is closed and $y^n \in \mu(x^n) \subset \gamma(x^n)$, $y \in \gamma(x)$. Suppose $y \notin \mu(x)$. Then there exists $z \in \gamma(x)$ with $z \in U(y,x)$. Since γ is lower hemi-continuous at x, by 11.11 there is a sequence $z^n \to z$, $z^n \in \gamma(x^n)$. Since U has open graph, $z^n \in U(y^n,x^n)$ eventually, which contradicts $y^n \in \mu(x^n)$. Thus μ is closed at x.

If γ is upper hemi-continuous as well since $\mu = \mu \cap \gamma$, and μ is closed at x, 11.21(b) implies that μ is upper hemi-continuous at x.

12.5 Proposition

Let $G \subset \mathbf{R}^m$, $Y \subset \mathbf{R}^k$ and let $U : G \times Y \twoheadrightarrow Y$ satisfy the following condition.

If $z \in U(y,x)$, then there is $z' \in U(y,x)$ such that $(y,x) \in int\ U^{-}[\{z'\}]$.

Define $\mu(x) = \{y \in Y : U(y,x) = \varnothing\}$. Then μ is closed.

12.6 Proof

Let $x^n \to x$, $y^n \in \mu(x^n)$, $y^n \to y$. Suppose $y \notin \mu(x)$. Then there must be $z \in U(y,x)$ and so by hypothesis there is some z' such that $(y,x) \in int\ U^{-}[\{z'\}]$. But then for n large enough, $z' \in U(y^n,x^n)$, which contradicts $y^n \in \mu(x^n)$.

12.7 Theorem (cf. Theorem 22.2, Walker [1979], Green [1984])

Let $X_i \subset \mathbf{R}^{k_i}$, $i = 1,...,n$ be compact and put $X = \prod_{i=1}^{n} X_i$. Let $G \subset \mathbf{R}^k$ and for each i, let $S_i : X \times G \twoheadrightarrow X_i$ be continuous with compact values and $U_i : X \times G \twoheadrightarrow X_i$ have open graph. Define $E : G \twoheadrightarrow X$ via

$$E(g) = \{x \in X : \text{for each } i,\ x_i \in S_i(x,g);\ U_i(x,g) \cap S_i(x,g) = \varnothing\}.$$

Then E has compact values, is closed and upper hemi-continuous.

12.8 Proof

By 11.9 it suffices to prove that E is closed, so suppose that $(g,x) \notin Gr\ E$. Then for some i, either $x_i \notin S_i(x,g)$ or $U_i(x,g) \cap S_i(x,g) \neq \varnothing$. By 11.9, S_i is closed and so in the first case a neighborhood of (x,g) is disjoint from $Gr\ E$. In the second case, let $z_i \in U_i(x,g) \cap S_i(x,g)$. Since U_i has open graph, there are neighborhoods V of z_i and W_1 of (x,g) such that $W \times V \subset Gr\ U_i$. Since S_i is lower hemi-continuous, there is a neighborhood W_2 of (x,g) such that $(x',g') \in W_2$ implies $S_i(x',g') \cap V \neq \varnothing$. Thus $W_1 \cap W_2$ is a neighborhood of (x,g) disjoint from $Gr\ E$. Thus $Gr\ E$ is closed.

12.9 Proposition

Let $K \subset \mathbf{R}^m$ be compact, $G \subset \mathbf{R}^k$, and let $\gamma : K \times G \twoheadrightarrow K$ be closed. Put $F(g) = \{x \in K : x \in \gamma(x,g)\}$. Then $F : G \twoheadrightarrow K$ has compact values, is closed and upper hemi-continuous.

12.10 Proof

It suffices to prove that F is closed, but this is immediate.

12.11 Proposition

Let $K \subset \mathbf{R}^m$ be compact, $G \subset \mathbf{R}^k$, and let $\gamma : K \times G \twoheadrightarrow \mathbf{R}^m$ be upper hemi-continuous and have compact values. Put $Z(g) = \{x \in K : 0 \in \gamma(x,g)\}$. Then $Z : G \twoheadrightarrow K$ has compact values, is closed and upper hemi-continuous.

12.12 Proof

Exercise.

CHAPTER 13

Approximation of correspondences

13.0 Remark

In Theorem 13.3 we show that we can approximate the graph of a nonempty and convex-valued closed correspondence by the graph of a continuous function, in the sense that for any $\varepsilon > 0$ the graph of the continuous function can be chosen to lie in an ε-neighborhood of the graph of the correspondence. This result is due to von Neumann [1937] and is fundamental in extending the earlier results for functions to correspondences.

13.1 Lemma (Cellina [1969])

Let $\gamma : E \twoheadrightarrow F$ be upper hemi-continuous and have nonempty compact convex values, where $E \subset \mathbf{R}^m$ is compact and $F \subset \mathbf{R}^k$ is convex. For $\delta > 0$ define γ^δ via $\gamma^\delta(x) = co \bigcup_{z \in N_\delta(x)} \gamma(z)$. Then for every $\varepsilon > 0$, there is a $\delta > 0$ such that

$$Gr\ \gamma^\delta \subset N_\varepsilon(Gr\ \gamma).$$

(Note that this does *not* say that $\gamma^\delta(x) \subset N_\varepsilon(\gamma(x))$ for all x.)

13.2 Proof

Suppose not. Then we must have a sequence (x^n,y^n) with $(x^n,y^n) \in Gr\ \gamma^{(\frac{1}{n})}$ such that $dist\ ((x^n,y^n), Gr\ \gamma) \geqslant \varepsilon > 0$. Now $(x^n,y^n) \in Gr\ \gamma^{(\frac{1}{n})}$ means

$$y^n \in \gamma^{(\frac{1}{n})}(x^n), \text{ so } y^n \in co \bigcup_{z \in N_{(\frac{1}{n})}(x^n)} \gamma(z).$$

By Caratheodory's theorem there exist

$$y^{0,n},\dots,y^{k,n} \in \bigcup_{z \in N_{(\frac{1}{n})}(x^n)} \gamma(z)$$

such that $y^n = \sum_{i=0}^{k} \lambda_i^n y^{i,n}$ with $\lambda^i \geqslant 0$, $\sum \lambda^i = 1$, and $y^{i,n} \in \gamma(z^{i,n})$ with

$|z^{i,n} - x^n| < \frac{1}{n}$. Since E is compact and γ is upper hemi-continuous, 11.11(a) implies that we can extract convergent sequences such that $x^n \to x$, $y^{i,n} \to y^i$, $\lambda_i^n \to \lambda_i$, $z^{i,n} \to x$ for all i, and $y = \sum_{i=0}^{k} \lambda_i y^i$ and $(x,y^i) \in Gr\ \gamma$ for all i. Since γ is convex-valued, $(x,y) \in Gr\ \gamma$, which contradicts $dist\ ((x^n,y^n), Gr\ \gamma) \geqslant \varepsilon$ for all n.

13.3 von Neumann's Approximation Lemma (von Neumann [1937])
Let $\gamma : E \twoheadrightarrow F$ be upper hemi-continuous with nonempty compact convex values, where $E \subset \mathbf{R}^m$ is compact and $F \subset \mathbf{R}^k$ is convex. Then for any $\varepsilon > 0$ there is a continuous function f such that $Gr\ f \subset N_\varepsilon(Gr\ \gamma)$.

13.4 Proof (cf. Hildenbrand and Kirman [1976, Lemma AIV.1])
By 13.1 there is a $\delta > 0$ such that the correspondence γ^δ satisfies $Gr\ \gamma^\delta \subset N_\varepsilon(Gr\ \gamma)$. Since E is compact, there exists $x^1,\ldots,x^n$ such that $\{N_\delta(x^i)\}$ is an open cover of E. Choose $y^i \in \gamma(x^i)$. Let $f^1\ldots f^n$ be a partition of unity subordinate to this cover and set $g(x) = \sum_{i=1}^{n} f^i(x) y^i$. Then g is continuous and since f^i vanishes outside $N_\delta(x^i)$, $f^i(x) > 0$ implies $|x^i - x| < \delta$ so $g(x) \in \gamma^\delta(x)$.

13.5 Note
The hypothesis of upper hemi-continuity of γ is essential, as can be seen by considering γ to be the indicator function of the rationals and $E = \mathbf{R}$.

CHAPTER 14

Selection theorems for correspondences

14.0 Remark
Theorems 14.3 and 14.7 are continuous selection theorems. That is, they assert the existence of a continuous function in the graph of a correspondence. Theorem 14.3 is due to Browder [1968, Theorem 1] and 14.7 is a special case of Michael [1956, Theorem 3.2"]. Michael's theorem is much stronger than the form stated here, which will be adequate for our purposes. The theorems say that a nonempty-valued correspondence admits a continuous selection if it has convex values and open lower sections or is lower hemi-continuous with closed convex values.

14.1 Definition
Let $\gamma : E \twoheadrightarrow F$. A *selection* from γ is a function $f : E \to F$ such that for every $x \in E$, $f(x) \in \gamma(x)$.

14.2 Note
Selections can only be made from nonempty-valued correspondences, hence for the remainder of this section *all correspondences will be assumed to be nonempty-valued.*

14.3 Theorem (Browder [1968, Theorem 1])
Let $E \subset \mathbf{R}^m$ and $\gamma : E \twoheadrightarrow \mathbf{R}^k$ have convex values and satisfy $\gamma^{-1}(y)$ is open for each y. Then there is a continuous $f : E \to \mathbf{R}^k$ such that $f(x) \in \gamma(x)$ for each x.

14.4 Proof (Browder [1968], cf. 7.3)
By 2.25 there is a locally finite partition of unity $\{f_y\}$ subordinate to $\{\gamma^{-1}(y)\}$, so $f(x) = \sum_y f_y(x)y$ is continuous. If $f_y(x) > 0$, then $y \in \gamma(x)$. Since γ is convex-valued, $f(x) \in \gamma(x)$.

14.5 Lemma (Michael [1956, Lemma 4.1], cf. (13.3))
Let $E \subset \mathbf{R}^m$ be compact and $\gamma : E \twoheadrightarrow \mathbf{R}^k$ be convex-valued and lower hemi-continuous. Let $\varepsilon > 0$ be given. Then there exists a continuous $f : E \to \mathbf{R}^k$ such that $f(x) \in N_\varepsilon(\gamma(x))$ for each $x \in E$.

14.6 Proof (Michael [1956])

For each $y \in \mathbf{R}^k$ let $W_y = \{x \in E : y \in N_\varepsilon(\gamma(x))\}$. Then $x \in \gamma^-[N_\varepsilon(\gamma(x))] \subset W_y$. Since γ is lower hemi-continuous, each W_y is open and hence the W_y's form an open cover of E. Thus there is a partition of unity $f^1,\ldots,f^n$ subordinate to $W_{y^1},\ldots,W_{y^n}$. Set $f(x) = \sum_{i=1}^{n} f^i(x)y^i$. Since $N_\varepsilon(\gamma(x))$ is convex and $f^i(x) > 0$ implies that $y_i \in N_\varepsilon(\gamma(x))$, we have $f(x) \in N_\varepsilon(\gamma(x))$ for each x.

14.7 Theorem (cf. Michael [1956, Theorem 3.2"])

Let $E \subset \mathbf{R}^m$ be compact and $\gamma : E \twoheadrightarrow \mathbf{R}^k$ be lower hemi-continuous with closed convex values. Then there is a continuous $f : E \to \mathbf{R}^k$ such that $f(x) \in \gamma(x)$ for each x.

14.8 Proof (Michael [1956])

Let V_n be the open ball of radius $1/2^n$ about $0 \in \mathbf{R}^k$. We will construct a sequence of functions $f^n : E \to \mathbf{R}^k$ such that for each x

(i) $f^n(x) \in f^{n-1}(x) + 2V_{n-1}$ and

(ii) $f^n(x) \in \gamma(x) + V^n$.

By (i) f^n is a uniformly Cauchy sequence and hence converges uniformly to a function f which must be continuous (Rudin [1976, 7.12]). From (ii) and the fact that $\gamma(x)$ is closed for each x we have $f(x) \in \gamma(x)$.

The sequence f^n is constructed by induction. A function f^1 satisfying (ii) exists by 14.5. Given $f^1,\ldots,f^n$ construct f^{n+1} by first defining γ_{n+1} via $\gamma_{n+1}(x) = \gamma(x) \cap (f^n(x) + V_n)$. By the induction hypothesis (ii) $\gamma_{n+1}(x)$ is nonempty and furthermore γ_{n+1} is lower hemi-continuous. (To see that γ_{n+1} is lower hemi-continuous, put $\mu(x) = f^n(x) + V_n$. Then μ is lower hemi-continuous since f^n is continuous. Then by 11.25 the correspondence $\gamma \times \mu$ is lower hemi-continuous and

$$\begin{aligned}\gamma_{n+1}^-[W] &= \{x : \gamma(x) \cap W \neq \varnothing;\ \mu(x) \cap W \neq \varnothing\}\\ &= \{x : \gamma \times \mu(x) \cap [V \cap (\mathbf{R}^k \times W)] \neq \varnothing\}\\ &= (\gamma \times \mu)^- \ [V \cap (\mathbf{R}^k \times W)]\end{aligned}$$

which is open, since $\gamma \times \mu$ is lower hemi-continuous.) Applying 14.3 to γ_{n+1} yields f^{n+1} with $f^{n+1}(x) \in \gamma_{n+1}(x) + V_{n+1}$ for each x. But then

$$f^{n+1}(x) \in f^n(x) + V_n + V_{n+1} \subset f^n(x) + 2V_n.$$

CHAPTER 15

Fixed point theorems for correspondences

15.0 Remarks

Since functions can be viewed as singleton-valued correspondences, Brouwer's fixed point theorem can be viewed as a fixed point theorem for continuous singleton-valued correspondences. The assumption of singleton values can be relaxed. A *fixed point* of a correspondence μ is a point x satisfying $x \in \mu(x)$.

Kakutani [1941] proved a fixed point theorem (Corollary 15.3) for closed correspondences with nonempty convex values mapping a compact convex set into itself. His theorem can be viewed as a useful special case of von Neumann's intersection lemma (16.4). (See 21.1.) A useful generalization of Kakutani's theorem is Theorem 15.1 below. Loosely speaking, the theorem says that if a correspondence mapping a compact convex set into itself is the continuous image of a closed correspondence with nonempty convex values into a compact convex set, then it has a fixed point. This theorem is a slight variant of a theorem of Cellina [1969] and the proof is based on von Neumann's approximation lemma (13.3) and the Brouwer fixed point theorem. Another generalization of Kakutani's theorem is due to Eilenberg and Montgomery [1946]. Their theorem is discussed in Section 15.8, and relies on algebraic topological notions beyond the scope of this text. While the Eilenberg-Montgomery theorem is occasionally quoted in the mathematical economics literature (e.g. Debreu [1952], Kuhn [1956], Mas-Colell [1974]), Theorem 15.1 seems general enough for many applications. (In particular see 21.5.)

The theorems above apply to closed correspondences into a compact set. Such correspondences are upper hemi-continuous by 11.9(b). There are also fixed point theorems for lower hemi-continuous correspondences (15.4 and 15.6.) The proofs of these theorems rely on selection theorems (14.3 and 14.7) and the Brouwer fixed point theorem.

15.1 Theorem (cf. Cellina [1969])
Let $K \subset \mathbf{R}^m$ be nonempty, compact and convex, and let $\mu : K \twoheadrightarrow K$. Suppose that there is a closed correspondence $\gamma : K \twoheadrightarrow F$ with nonempty compact convex values, where $F \subset \mathbf{R}^k$ is compact and convex, and a continuous $f : K \times F \to K$ such that for each $x \in K$

$$\mu(x) = \{f(x,y) : y \in \gamma(x)\}.$$

Then μ has a fixed point, i.e., there is some $x \in K$ satisfying $x \in \mu(x)$.

15.2 Proof (cf. Cellina [1969])
By 13.3 there is a sequence of functions $g^n : K \to F$ such that $Gr\ g^n \in N_{\frac{1}{n}}(Gr\ \gamma)$. Define $h^n : K \to K$ by $h^n(x) = f(x,g^n(x))$. By Brouwer's theorem each h^n has a fixed point x^n, i.e., $x^n = f(x^n,g^n(x^n))$. As K and F are compact we can extract a convergent subsequence; so without loss of generality, assume $x^n \to \bar{x}$ and $g^n(x^n) \to \bar{y}$. Then $(\bar{x},\bar{y}) \in Gr\ \gamma$ as γ is closed and so $\bar{x} = f(\bar{x},\bar{y}) \in \mu(\bar{x})$.

15.3 Corollary (Kakutani [1941])
Let $K \subset \mathbf{R}^m$ be compact and convex and $\gamma : K \twoheadrightarrow K$ be closed or upper hemi-continuous with nonempty convex compact values. Then γ has a fixed point.

15.4 Theorem
Let $K \subset \mathbf{R}^m$ be compact and convex and let $\gamma : K \twoheadrightarrow K$ be lower hemi-continuous and have closed convex values. Then γ has a fixed point.

15.5 Proof
Immediate from the selection theorem (14.7) and Brouwer's theorem (6.5).

15.6 Theorem (Browder [1968])
Let $K \subset \mathbf{R}^m$ be compact and convex and let $\gamma : K \twoheadrightarrow K$ have nonempty convex values and satisfy $\gamma^{-1}(y)$ is open for all $y \in K$. Then γ has a fixed point.

15.7 Proof
Immediate from the selection theorem (14.3) and Brouwer's theorem (6.5).

15.8 Remarks
The Eilenberg-Montgomery theorem relies for its general statement on ideas which will not be taken up here. Thus some terms will remain undefined in this discussion. Their definitions may be found in

Borsuk [1967]. A set is called *acyclic* if it has all the same homology groups as a singleton. (Borsuk [1967, p. 35].) (This has nothing to do with acyclic binary relations as discussed in Chapter 7.) A sufficient condition for a set to be acyclic is for it to be contractible to a point belonging to it. A set E is *contractible* to $\bar{x} \in E$ if there is a continuous function $h : E \times [0,1] \to E$ satisfying $h(x,0) = x$ for all x and $h(x,1) = \bar{x}$ for all x. Convex sets are clearly contractible. (Set $h(x,t) = (1 - t)x + t\bar{x}$.) An *ANR* is a compact r-image (6.8) of an open subset of the Hilbert cube. (Borsuk [1967, p. 100].) A *polyhedron* is a finite union of closed simplexes. A finite-dimensional ANR is an r-image of a polyhedron. (Borsuk [1967, pp. 11, 122]).

15.9 Theorem (Eilenberg and Montgomery [1946])
Let $E \subset \mathbf{R}^m$ be an acyclic ANR and $\gamma : E \twoheadrightarrow E$ be closed with nonempty compact acyclic values. Then γ has a fixed point.

CHAPTER 16

Sets with convex sections and a minimax theorem

16.0 Remarks

In this chapter we present results on intersections of sets with convex sections and apply them to proving minimax theorems. Further applications are given in Chapter 21. Theorem 16.2 was proven by von Neumann [1937] for the case $n = 2$. The general case is due to Fan [1952], using a technique due to Kakutani [1941]. For convenience, the case $n = 2$ is written separately as Corollary 16.4. Theorem 16.1 says that given closed sets $E_1,\ldots,E_n$ in a product $\prod_{i=1}^{n} X_i$, if they have appropriate convex sections, then their intersection is nonempty. Theorem 16.5 derives a similar conclusion, but the closedness assumption on the sets is replaced by an open section condition. This theorem is due to Fan [1964]. Fan's proof is based on his generalization of the K-K-M lemma (5.7). The proof given here is due to Browder [1968]. Corollary 16.7 is virtually a restatement of Theorem 16.5 in terms of real-valued functions, but has as a relatively simple consequence a very general minimax theorem (16.9) due to Sion [1958]. The proof here is due to Fan [1964]. Sion's theorem is a minimax theorem for functions which are quasi-concave and upper semi-continuous in one variable and quasi-convex and lower semi-continuous in the other. It includes as a special case von Neumann's [1928] celebrated minimax theorem for bilinear functions defined on a product of two closed simplexes. Von Neumann's theorem can be proven using the separating hyperplane theorem without using fixed point methods. Another minimax theorem (16.11) is due to Fan [1972]. It dispenses with upper semi-continuity and quasi-convexity and returns a different sort of conclusion and is a very powerful result. (See 21.10-12.)

16.1 Notation

For $i = 1,\ldots,n$, let $X_i \subset \mathbf{R}^{k_i}$. Set $X = \prod_{i=1}^{n} X_i$ and $X_{-i} = \prod_{j \neq i} X_j$. For

$x \in X$ denote by x_{-i} the projection of x on X_{-i}. Given $x_{-i} \in X_{-i}$ and $y_i \in X_i$, let (x_{-i},y_i) be the vector in X whose ith component is x_i and whose projection on X_{-i} is x_i. For $E \subset X$, let

$$E^{-1}(y_i) = \{x_{-i} \in X_{-i} : (x_{-i},y_i) \in E\}$$

and

$$E^{-1}(x_{-i}) = \{y_i \in X_i : (x_{-i},y_i) \in E\}.$$

16.2 Theorem (Fan [1952], von Neumann [1937])
For $i = 1,...,n$, let $X_i \subset \mathbf{R}^{k_i}$ be compact and convex and let E_i be closed subsets of X satisfying

for every $x_{-i} \in X_{-i}$, $E_i^{-1}(x_{-i})$ is convex and nonempty.

Then $\bigcap_{i=1}^{n} E_i$ is nonempty and compact.

16.3 16.3 Proof (Fan [1952], Kakutani [1941]).
Compactness is immediate. Define the correspondences $\gamma_i : X_{-i}$ by $Gr\ \gamma_i = E_i$. Define $\gamma : X \twoheadrightarrow X$ by $\gamma(x) = \prod_{i=1}^{n} \gamma_i(x_{-i})$. This correspondence has closed graph and nonempty convex values and so satisfies the hypotheses of Kakutani's fixed point theorem (15.3). But the set of fixed points of γ is exactly $\bigcap_{i=1}^{n} E_i$.

16.4 Corollary: von Neumann's Intersection Lemma (von Neumann [1937])
Let $X \subset \mathbf{R}^m$, $Y \subset \mathbf{R}^n$ be compact and convex, and let E,F be closed subsets of $X \times Y$ satisfying

for every $x \in X$, $E_x = \{y : (x,y) \in E\}$ is convex and nonempty,

and

for every $y \in Y$, $F_y = \{x : (x,y) \in F\}$ is convex and nonempty.

Then $E \cap F$ is nonempty and compact.

16.5 Theorem (Fan [1964])
For $i = 1,...,n$, let $X_i \subset \mathbf{R}^{k_i}$ be compact and convex and let E_i be subsets of X satisfying

for every $x_{-i} \in X_{-i}$, $E_i^{-1}(x_{-i})$ is convex and nonempty.

and

for every $x_i \in X_i$, $E_i^{-1}(x_i)$ is open in X_{-i}.

Then $\bigcap_{i=1}^{n} E_i$ is nonempty.

16.6 Proof (Browder [1968, Theorem 11])
Define the correspondences $\gamma_i : X_{-i}$ by $Gr\ \gamma_i = E_i$. Define $\gamma : X \twoheadrightarrow X$ by $\gamma(x) = \prod_{i=1}^{n} \gamma_i(x_{-i})$. The correspondence γ has convex values and $\gamma^{-1}(x) = \bigcap_{i=1}^{n} (E_i^{-1}(x_i) \times X_i)$, which is open. Therefore by 15.6, γ has a fixed point, but the set of fixed points of γ is exactly $\bigcap_{i=1}^{n} E_i$.

16.7 Corollary (Fan [1964])
For $i = 1,\ldots,n$, let $X_i \subset \mathbf{R}^{k_i}$ and let $f_i : X \to \mathbf{R}$. Assume that for each x_{-i}, f_i is quasi-concave as a function on X_i; and that for each x_i, f_i is lower semi-continuous as a function on X_{-i}. Let $\alpha_1,\ldots,\alpha_n$ be real numbers such that for each $x_{-i} \in X_{-i}$, there is a $y_i \in X_i$ satisfying $f(x_{-i},y_i) > \alpha_i$. Then there is an $\bar{x} \in X$ satisfying $f_i(\bar{x}) > \alpha_i$ for all i.

16.8 Proof
Let $E_i = \{x \in X : f_i(x) > \alpha_i\}$. Then the hypotheses of 16.6 are satisfied, so $\bigcap_{i=1}^{n} E_i \neq \varnothing$.

16.9 Theorem (Sion [1958])
Let $X \subset \mathbf{R}^m$, $Y \subset \mathbf{R}^n$ be compact and convex and let $f : X \times Y \to \mathbf{R}$. Assume that for each fixed $x \in X$, f is lower semi-continuous and quasi-convex on Y; and for each fixed $y \in Y$, f is upper semi-continuous and quasi-concave on X. Then

$$\min_{y\in Y} \max_{x\in X} f(x,y) = \max_{x\in X} \min_{y\in Y} f(x,y).$$

16.10 Proof (Fan [1964])
Clearly, for any $\varepsilon > 0$, for any $\bar{y} \in Y$ there is some $\bar{x} \in X$ satisfying

$$f(\bar{x},\bar{y}) > \min_{y\in Y} \max_{x\in X} f(x,y) - \varepsilon$$

and for any $\bar{x} \in X$ there is some $\bar{y} \in Y$ satisfying

$$f(\bar{x},\bar{y}) < \max_{x\in X} \min_{y\in Y} f(x,y) + \varepsilon.$$

Set $f_1 = f$, $f_2 = -f$, $\alpha_1 = \min_{y\in Y} \max_{x\in X} f(x,y) - \varepsilon$, and $\alpha_2 = -(\max_{x\in X} \min_{y\in Y} f(x,y) + \varepsilon)$. Then the hypotheses of 16.7 are satisfied and so there is some $(x_\varepsilon,y_\varepsilon)$ satisfying

$$\min_{y\in Y} \max_{x\in X} f(x,y) - \varepsilon < f(x_\varepsilon,y_\varepsilon) < \max_{x\in X} \min_{y\in Y} f(x,y) + \varepsilon.$$

Letting $\varepsilon \downarrow 0$ yields the conclusion.

16.11 Theorem (Fan [1972])
Let $K \subset \mathbf{R}^m$ be compact and convex. Let $F : K \times K \to \mathbf{R}$ be lower semi-continuous in its second argument and quasi-concave in its first argument. Then

$$\min_{y \varepsilon K} \sup_{z \varepsilon K} f(z,g) \leqslant \sup_{x \varepsilon K} f(x,x).$$

16.12 Proof (Fan [1972])
Let $\alpha = \sup_{x \varepsilon K} f(x,x)$. Define a binary relation U on K by

$$z \in U(y) \text{ if and only if } f(z,y) > \alpha.$$

Since f is quasi-concave in its first argument $U(y)$ is convex for each y and since f is lower semi-continuous in its second argument $U^{-1}(z)$ is open for each z. Also $f(z,z) \leqslant \alpha$, so $z \notin U(z)$. By 7.2 U has a maximal element $\bar{y}$. Thus $f(z,\bar{y}) \leqslant \alpha$ for all z, i.e., $\sup_{z \varepsilon K} f(z,\bar{y}) \leqslant \alpha$, so $\min_{y \varepsilon K} \sup_{z \varepsilon K} f(z,y) \leqslant \sup_{x \varepsilon K} f(x,x)$.

CHAPTER 17

The Fan-Browder theorem

17.0 Remarks

The theorems of this chapter can be viewed as generalizations of fixed point theorems. Theorem 17.1 is due to Fan [1969] and is based on a theorem of Browder [1967]. It gives conditions on correspondences $\mu, \gamma : K \to \mathbf{R}^m$ which guarantee the existence of an $x \in K$ satisfying $\mu(x) \cap \gamma(x) \neq \emptyset$. Browder proves the theorem for the special case in which μ is a singleton-valued correspondence and γ is the identity correspondence. In this case $\mu(x) \cap \gamma(x) \neq \emptyset$ if and only if x is a fixed point of μ. The correspondences are not required to map K into itself; instead, a rather peculiar looking condition is used. In the case studied by Browder, this condition says that μ is either an *inward* or an *outward* map. Such conditions were studied by Halpern [1968] and Halpern and Bergman [1968].

Another feature of these theorems, also due more or less to Browder, is the combination of a separating hyperplane argument with a maximization argument. The maximization argument is based on 7.2; which is equivalent to a fixed point argument. Such a form of argument is also used in 18.18 below and is implicit in 21.6 and 21.7.

17.1 Fan-Browder Theorem (Fan [1969, Theorem 6])

Let $K \subset \mathbf{R}^m$ be compact and convex, and let $\gamma,\mu : K \twoheadrightarrow \mathbf{R}^m$ be upper hemi-continuous with nonempty closed convex values. Assume that for each $x \in K$ at least one of $\mu(x)$ or $\gamma(x)$ is compact. Suppose that for each $x \in K$ there exist three points $y \in K$, $u \in \gamma(x)$, $v \in \mu(x)$ and a real number $\lambda > 0$ such that $y = x + \lambda(u - v)$. (See Figure 17.) Then there is $z \in K$ satisfying $\gamma(z) \cap \mu(z) \neq \emptyset$.

17.2 Proof (cf. Fan [1969])

Suppose the conclusion fails, i.e., suppose $\gamma(x)$ and $\mu(x)$ are disjoint for each $x \in K$. Then by the separating hyperplane theorem (2.9), the correspondence P defined by

$$P(x) = \{p \in \mathbf{R}^m : \exists c \in \mathbf{R} \quad p \cdot \mu(x) > c > p \cdot \gamma(x)\}$$

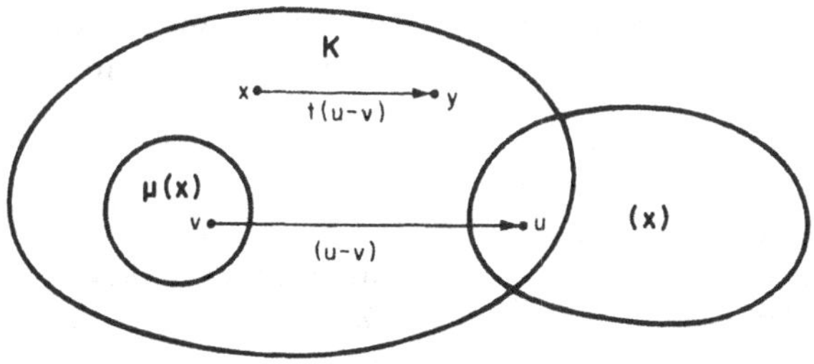

Figure 17

has nonempty values for each x. Each $P(x)$ is clearly convex. In addition, $P^{-1}(p)$ is open for each p: Let $x \in P^{-1}(p)$. That is, $p \cdot \mu(x) > c > p \cdot \gamma(x)$. Since γ and μ are upper hemi-continuous,

$$\mu^+[\{z : p \cdot z > c\}] \cap \gamma^+[\{z : p \cdot z < c\}]$$

is a neighborhood of x contained in $P^{-1}(p)$. Thus by 14.3 there is a continuous selection p from P, i.e., p satisfies

$$p(x) \cdot \gamma(x) < p(x) \cdot \mu(x) \quad \text{for each } x \in K. \tag{17.3}$$

Define the binary relation U on K by $y \in U(x)$ if and only if $p(x) \cdot x > p(x) \cdot y$. Then U has open graph as p is continuous. For each $x \in K$, U(x) is convex (or empty) and $x \notin U(x)$. Thus by Fan's lemma (7.5), there is a point x^0 such that $U(x^0) = \varnothing$, i.e.,

$$p(x^0) \cdot y \geqslant p(x^0) \cdot x^0 \quad \text{for all } y \in K. \tag{17.4}$$

By hypothesis there exist $y^0 \in K$, $u^0 \in \gamma(x^0)$, $v^0 \in \mu(x^0)$ and $\lambda > 0$ such that

$$y^0 = x^0 + \lambda(u^0 - v^0)$$

so by 17.4

$$\lambda p(x^0) \cdot u^0 \geqslant \lambda p(x^0) \cdot v^0;$$

which contradicts 17.3. Thus there must be some point z with $\gamma(z) \cap \mu(z) \neq \varnothing$.

17.5 Remark

A perhaps more intuitive form of Theorem 17.1 is given in the next theorem. The proof rearranges the order of the ideas used in 17.2. The relationship between the two theorems can be seen by setting $\beta(x) = \gamma(x) - \mu(x)$, and noting that $0 \in \beta(x)$ if and only if $\gamma(x) \cap \mu(x) \neq \varnothing$. Theorem 17.6 can be interpreted as saying that if an upper hemi-continuous set-valued vector field always has a vector which points inward on a compact convex set, then it must vanish somewhere in the set.

17.6 Theorem

Let $K \subset \mathbf{R}^m$ be compact and convex, and let $\beta : K \twoheadrightarrow \mathbf{R}^m$ be an upper hemi-continuous correspondence with nonempty closed convex values satisfying the following condition. For each $x \in K$, there exists $\lambda > 0$ and $w \in \beta(x)$ such that

$$x + \lambda w \in K.$$

Then there is $z \in K$ satisfying $0 \in \beta(z)$.

17.7 Proof

Suppose not. Then by 2.9, for each x we can strictly separate 0 and $\beta(x)$, i.e., there exists some p_x such that $p_x \cdot \beta(x) > 0$. From 14.3 it follows as in 17.2, that there exists a continuous $p : K \to \mathbf{R}^m$ such that

$$p(x) \cdot \beta(x) > 0 \text{ for all } x \in K. \tag{17.8}$$

By 8.1 there exists $\bar{x} \in K$ satisfying

$$p(\bar{x}) \cdot \bar{x} \geqslant p(\bar{x}) \cdot x \text{ for all } x \in K. \tag{17.9}$$

But by hypothesis there is some $\lambda > 0$ and $w \in \beta(\bar{x})$ such that $\bar{x} + \lambda w \in K$. Substituting $\bar{x} + \lambda w$ for x in 17.9 gives $p(\bar{x}) \cdot w \leqslant 0$, contradicting 17.8.

17.10 Note

In the statements of both Theorems 17.1 and 17.6, the condition $\lambda > 0$ can be replaced by $\lambda < 0$.

CHAPTER 18

Equilibrium of excess demand correspondences

18.0 Remarks

The following theorem is fundamental to proving the existence of a market equilibrium of an economy and generalizes Theorem 8.3 to the case of set-valued excess demand correspondences. In this case, if γ is the excess demand correspondence, then p is an *equilibrium price* if $0 \in \gamma(p)$. The price p is a *free disposal equilibrium price* if there is a $z \in \gamma(p)$ such that $z \leqslant 0$.

Theorem 12.3 can be used to show that demand correspondences are upper hemi-continuous if certain restrictions on endowments are met. In the case of complete convex preferences, the demand correspondences have convex values. The supply correspondences can be shown to be upper hemi-continuous by means of Theorem 12.1 (Berge's maximum theorem). Much of the difficulty in proving the existence of an equilibrium comes in proving that we may take the excess demand correspondence to be compact-valued. (See, e.g., Debreu [1962].) In the case where preferences are not complete, which is the point of Theorem 12.3, we cannot guarantee that the excess demand correspondence will be convex-valued. In such cases, different techniques are required. These are discussed in Chapter 22 below.

18.1 Theorem: Gale-Debreu-Nikaido Lemma (Gale [1955]; Kuhn [1956]; Nikaido [1956]; Debreu [1956])

Let $\gamma : \Delta \twoheadrightarrow \mathbf{R}^m$ be an upper hemi-continuous correspondence with nonempty compact convex values such that for all $p \in \Delta$

$$p \cdot z \leqslant 0 \text{ for each } z \in \gamma(p).$$

Put $N = -\mathbf{R}_+^{n+1}$. Then $\{p \in \Delta : N \cap \gamma(p) \neq \varnothing\}$ of free disposal equilibrium prices is nonempty and compact.

18.2 Proof

For each $p \in \Delta$ set

$$U(p) = \{q : q \cdot z > 0 \text{ for all } z \in \gamma(p)\}.$$

Then $U(p)$ is convex for each p and $p \notin U(p)$, and we have that $U^{-1}(p)$ is open for each p:

For if $q \in U^{-1}(p)$, we have that $p \cdot z > 0$ for all $z \in \gamma(q)$. Then since γ is upper hemi-continuous, $\gamma^{+}[\{x : p \cdot x > 0\}]$ is a neighborhood of q in $U^{-1}(p)$.

Now p is U-maximal if and only if

$$\text{for each } q \in \Delta, \text{ there is a } z \in \gamma(p) \text{ with } q \cdot z \leqslant 0.$$

By 2.15, p is U-maximal if and only if $\gamma(p) \cap N \neq \emptyset$. Thus by 7.2, $\{p : \gamma(p) \cap N \neq \emptyset\}$ is nonempty and compact.

18.3 Proposition

Let C be a closed convex cone in $\mathbf{R}^m$ and set $D = C \cap \{p : |p| = 1\}$. Then D is homeomorphic to a compact convex set if and only if C is not a linear space.

18.4 Proof

Suppose C is not a linear subspace. Then by 2.18, $C^{*} \cap -C \neq \{0\}$. Let $u \neq 0$ belong to $C^{*} \cap -C$. Then $z = \dfrac{-u}{|u|} \in D$ and $p \cdot z \geqslant 0$ for all $p \in C$. As a result $-z \notin C$. (For $-z \cdot z < 0$.) Let $H = \{x : z \cdot x = 0\}$ be the hyperplane orthogonal to z and let $h : \mathbf{R}^m \to H$ be the orthogonal projection onto H, i.e., $h(p) = p - (p \cdot z)z$. The function h is linear and so continuous.

It is also true that h restricted to D is injective: Let $p,q \in D$ and suppose $h(p) = h(q)$. Then $p = q + \lambda z$ where $\lambda = (p-q) \cdot z$. Since $|p| = |q| = |z| = 1$, either $\lambda = 0$, in which case $p = q$; or either $p = z$, $q = -z$, $\lambda = 2$ or $p = -z$, $q = z$, $\lambda = -2$, both of which violate $-z \notin C$. Thus h is injective on D.

Since h is injective on D, which is compact, h is a homeomorphism between D and $h(D)$. (Rudin [1976], 4.17.) It remains to be shown that $h(D)$ is convex. Let $h(p) = x$, $h(q) = y$ for some $p,q \in D$. Since h is linear and $h(z) = 0$, $h(\lambda p + (1-\lambda)q + \alpha z) = \lambda x + (1-\lambda)y$. Since $|p| = |q| = 1$, $|\lambda p + (1-\lambda)q| \leqslant 1$. Thus for some nonnegative value of α, $|\lambda p + (1-\lambda)q + \alpha z| = 1$. Since $p,q,z \in C$ and C is closed under addition (1.12(d)), $[\lambda p + (1-\lambda)q + \alpha z] \in D$ for $\lambda \in [0,1]$, $\alpha \geqslant 0$. Thus $\lambda x + (1-\lambda)y \in h(D)$.

Now suppose that C is a linear subspace, so that $C^{*} \cap -C = \{0\}$ (2.17). Then for each $x \in D$, $-x \notin C^{*}$; so by the separating hyperplane theorem (2.9), the correspondence P defined by

$$P(x) = \{p \in \mathbf{R}^n : p \cdot C^* \leqslant 0 < p \cdot (-x)\} = \{p \in C : p \cdot x < 0\}$$

has nonempty values. It is easy to verify that P satisfies the hypotheses of 14.3, so that there is a continuous function $p : D \to C$ satisfying $p(x) \cdot x < 0$. In particular, $p(x)$ is never zero. Thus the normalized function $\tilde{p} = \dfrac{p(x)}{|p(x)|}$ is continuous, maps D into itself and also satisfies $\tilde{p}(x) \cdot x < 0$ for every $x \in D$. Since $x \cdot x = 1 > 0$ for $x \in D$, p can have no fixed point. Therefore by Brouwer's theorem (6.9), D is not homeomorphic to a compact convex set.

18.5 Remark

The following theorem generalizes 18.1 in two ways. First, the domain can be generalized to be an arbitrary cone. If the correspondence is positively homogeneous of degree zero, then a compact domain is gotten by normalizing the prices to lie on the unit sphere. The condition for free disposal equilibrium is that some excess demand belong to the dual cone. The case where the domain is Δ corresponds to the cone being the nonnegative orthant. This generalization is due to Debreu [1956]. The second generalization is in relaxing Walras' law slightly. The new theorem requires only that $p \cdot z \leqslant 0$ for *some* $z \in \gamma(p)$, not for all of them. This generalization may be found in McCabe [1981] or Geistdoerfer-Florenzano [1982].

18.6 Theorem (cf. Debreu [1956])

Let C be a closed convex cone in $\mathbf{R}^m$, which is not a linear space. Let $D = C \cap \{p : |p| = 1\}$. Let $\gamma : D \twoheadrightarrow \mathbf{R}^m$ be an upper hemicontinuous correspondence with compact convex values satisfying:

for all $p \in D$, there is a $z \in \gamma(p)$ with $p \cdot z \leqslant 0$.

Then $\{p \in D : \gamma(p) \cap C^* \neq \varnothing\}$ is nonempty and compact.

18.7 Proof

Exercise. Hint: Define h as in 18.4 and set $K = h(D)$. Define the binary relation U on K by $q \in U(p)$ if and only if $h^{-1}(q) \cdot z > 0$ for all $z \in \gamma(h^{-1}(p))$. The rest of the proof follows 18.2.

18.8 Example

Let $C \subset \mathbf{R}^3 = \{p : p_3 = 0\}$, then $C^* = \{p : p_1 = 0; p_2 = 0\}$. For $p \in C \cap \{p : |p| = 1\}$ let $\gamma(p) = \{-p\}$. Then γ is an upper hemicontinuous correspondence with nonempty compact convex values which satisfies Walras' law, but for all $p \in C \cap \{p : |p| = 1\}$, $\gamma(p) \cap C^* = \varnothing$.

18.9 Remark

Two variations of Theorem 18.1 are given in Theorems 18.10 and 18.13 below, which are analogues of Theorem 8.7 for correspondences. These theorems give conditions for the existence of an equilibrium, rather than just a free disposal equilibrium. To do this, we use the boundary conditions (B2) and (B3), which are versions of (B1) for correspondences. Condition (B2) is used by Neuefeind [1980] and (B3) is used by Grandmont [1977]. Both theorems assume the strong form of Walras' law. Theorem 18.10 assumes that γ takes on closed values, while Theorem 18.13 assumes compact values.

18.10 Theorem (cf. Neuefeind [1980, Lemma 2])

Let $S = \{p \in \mathbf{R}^m : p > 0; \sum_{i=1}^{m} = 1\}$. Let $\gamma : S \twoheadrightarrow \mathbf{R}^m$ be upper hemi-continuous with nonempty closed convex values and satisfy the strong from of Walras' law and the boundary condition (B2):

(SWL) $p \cdot z = 0$ for all $z \in \gamma(p)$.

(B2) there is a $p^* \in S$ and a neighborhood V of $\Delta \setminus S$ in Δ such that for all $p \in V \cap S$, $p^* \cdot z > 0$ for all $z \in \gamma(p)$.

Then the set $\{p \in S : 0 \in \gamma(p)\}$ of equilibrium prices for γ is compact and nonempty.

18.11 Proof

Define the binary relation U on Δ by

$$p \in U(q) \text{ if } \begin{cases} p \cdot z > 0 \text{ for all } z \in \gamma(q) \text{ and } p,q \in S \\ \qquad \text{or} \\ p \in S,\ q \in \Delta \setminus S. \end{cases}$$

First show that the U-maximal elements are precisely the equilibrium prices. Suppose that $\bar{p}$ is U-maximal, i.e., $U(\bar{p}) = \varnothing$. Since $U(p) = S$ for all $p \in \Delta \setminus S$, it follows that $\bar{p} \in S$. Since $\bar{p} \in S$ and $U(\bar{p}) = \varnothing$,

$$\text{for each } q \in S, \text{ there is } a\ z \in \gamma(\bar{p}) \text{ with } q \cdot z \leqslant 0. \qquad 18.12$$

Now 18.12 implies $0 \in \gamma(\bar{p})$: Suppose by way of contradiction that $0 \notin \gamma(\bar{p})$. Then since $\{0\}$ is compact and convex and $\gamma(\bar{p})$ is closed and convex, by 2.9 there is $\tilde{p} \in \mathbf{R}^m$ satisfying $\tilde{p} \cdot z > 0$ for all $z \in \gamma(\bar{p})$. Put $p^\lambda = \lambda\tilde{p} + (1 - \lambda)\bar{p}$. Then for $z \in \gamma(\bar{p})$, $p^\lambda \cdot z = \lambda\tilde{p} \cdot z + (1 - \lambda)\bar{p} \cdot z = \lambda\tilde{p} \cdot z > 0$ for $\lambda > 0$. (Recall that $\bar{p} \cdot z = 0$ for $z \in \gamma(\bar{p})$ by Walras' law.) For $\lambda > 0$ small enough, $p^\lambda > 0$ so that the normalized price vector $q^\lambda = (\sum p_i^\lambda)^{-1} p^\lambda \in S$ and $q^\lambda \cdot z > 0$ for all $z \in \gamma(\bar{p})$, which violates 18.12.

Conversely, if $\bar{p}$ is an equilibrium price, then $0 \in \gamma(\bar{p})$ and since

$p \cdot 0 = 0$ for all p, it follows that $U(\bar{p}) = \varnothing$.

Next verify that U satisfies the hypotheses of Theorem 7.2:

(ia) $p \notin U(p)$: For $p \in S$ this follows from Walras' law. For $p \in \Delta \setminus S$, $p \notin S = U(p)$.

(ib) $U(p)$ is convex: For $p \in S$, let $q^1, q^2 \in q(p)$, i.e., $q^1 \cdot z > 0$, $q^2 \cdot z > 0$ for $z \in \gamma(p)$. Then $[\lambda q^1 + (1 - \lambda)q^2] \cdot z > 0$ as well. For $p \in \Delta \setminus S$, $U(p) = S$ which is convex.

(ii) If $q \in U^{-1}(p)$, then there is a p' with $q \in int\ U^{-1}(p')$: There are two cases: (a) $q \in S$ and (b) $q \in \Delta \setminus S$.

(iia) $q \in S \cap U^{-1}(p)$. Then $p \cdot z > 0$ for all $z \in \gamma(q)$. Let $H = \{x : p \cdot x > 0\}$, which is open. Then by upper hemi-continuity, $\gamma^+[H]$ is a neighborhood of q contained in $U^{-1}(p)$.

(iib) $q \in (\Delta \setminus S) \cap U^{-1}(p)$. By boundary condition (B2), $q \in int\ U^{-1}(p^*)$.

18.13 Theorem (cf. Grandmont [1977, Lemma 1])

Let $S = \{p \in \mathbf{R}^m : p > 0; \sum_{i=0}^{m} = 1\}$. Let $\gamma : S \twoheadrightarrow \mathbf{R}^m$ be upper hemi-continuous with nonempty compact convex values and satisfy the strong from of Walras' law and the boundary condition (B3):

(SWL) $p \cdot z = 0$ for all $z \in \gamma(p)$.

(B3) for every sequence $q^n \to q \in \Delta \setminus S$ and $z^n \in \gamma(q^n)$, there is a $p \in S$ (which may depend on $\{z^n\}$) such that $p \cdot z^n > 0$ for infinitely many n.

Then γ has an equilibrium price $\bar{p}$, i.e., $0 \in \gamma(\bar{p})$.

18.14 Proof

Exercise. Hint: Set $K_n = co\ \{x \in S : dist\ (x, \Delta \setminus S) \geqslant \frac{1}{n}\}$. Then $\{K_n\}$ is an increasing family of compact convex sets and $S = \bigcup_n K_n$. Let C_n be the cone generated by K_n. Use Theorem 18.6 to conclude that for each n, there is $q^n \in K_n$ such that $\gamma(q^n) \cap C_n^* \neq \varnothing$. Let $z^n \in \gamma(q^n) \cap C_n^*$.

Suppose that $q^n \to q \in \Delta \setminus S$. Then by the boundary condition (B3), there is a $p \in S$ such that $p \cdot z^n > 0$ infinitely often. But for large enough n, $p \in K_n \subset C_n$. Since $z^n \in C_n^*$, it follows that $p \cdot z^n \leqslant 0$, a contradiction.

It follows then that no subsequence of q^n converges to a point in $\Delta \setminus S$. Since Δ is compact, some subsequence must converge to some $\bar{p} \in S$. Since γ is upper hemi-continuous with compact values, by 11.11(a) there is a subsequence of z^n converging to $\bar{z} \in \gamma(\bar{p})$. This $\bar{z}$ lies in $\bigcap_n C_n^* = -\mathbf{R}^m_+$. This fact together with the strong form of Walras' law imply that $\bar{z} = 0$.

18.15 Remark

The boundary conditions (B2) and (B3) do not look at all similar on the face of them. However, (B2) is equivalent to the following condition (B2'), which is clearly stronger than (B3).

(B2') There is a $p^* \in S$ such that for every sequence $q^n \to q \in \Delta \setminus S$, there is an M such that for every $n \geqslant M$,

$$p^* \cdot z > 0 \text{ for all } z \in \gamma(q^n).$$

It is easy to see that (B2') follows from (B2) for if $q^n \to q \in \Delta \setminus S$, then there is some M such that for all $n \geqslant M$, $q^n \in V$. Suppose that γ satisfies (B2'). Let $V = \gamma^+[\{z : p^* \cdot z > 0\}]$. Since γ is upper hemi-continuous, V is open in S. Let $q^n \to q \in \Delta \setminus S$. By (B2') there is an M such that $n \geqslant M$ implies $q^n \in V$. This means that $V \cup (\Delta \setminus S)$ must be open in Δ.

The boundary condition (B3) is weaker than (B2') because in effect it allows p^* to depend on $\{q^n\}$ and $\{z^n\}$ and not to be fixed. Theorem 18.13 is *not* stronger than 18.10 as a result because 18.13 requires γ to have compact values and 18.10 assumes only closed values. This apparent advantage of Theorem 18.13 is of little practical consequence, as in most economic applications the correspondences will have compact values. Neuefeind [1980] presents an example which he attributes to P. Artzner, that shows that (B3) is indeed weaker than (B2).

18.16 Remark

Theorem 18.6 allows the domain to be a convex cone that is not a subspace. The problem with the economic interpretation of having a linear subspace of price vectors is defining the excess demand at the zero price vector. Nevertheless Bergstrom [1976] has found a clever modification of the excess demand correspondence which is useful in proving the existence of a Walrasian equilibrium without assuming that goods may be freely disposed. Mathematically, Theorem 18.6 can be extended to cover the case of a linear subspace at the cost of having to define the excess demand at the zero price vector and allowing the zero vector to be the free disposal equilibrium price. The theorem below is due to Geistdoerfer-Florenzano [1982].

18.17 Theorem (Geistdoerfer-Florenzano [1982])

Let C be a closed convex cone in $\mathbf{R}^m$, $B = \{p : |p| \leqslant 1\}$ and $\gamma : B \cap C \twoheadrightarrow \mathbf{R}^m$ be an upper hemi-continuous correspondence with nonempty compact convex values satisfying:

$$\text{if } |p| = 1, \text{ then there is a } z \in \gamma(p) \text{ with } p \cdot z \leqslant 0. \qquad 18.17.1$$

Then $\{p \in B : \gamma(p) \cap C^*\}$ is compact and nonempty.

18.18 Proof (Geistdoerfer-Florenzano [1982])
Compactness is routine. Suppose the nonemptiness assertion is false. Then as in 17.2, there is a continuous function $\pi : B \cap C \twoheadrightarrow \mathbf{R}^m$ satisfying $\pi(p) \cdot \gamma(p) > \pi(p) \cdot C^*$. By 2.14(c), $\pi(p) \cdot \gamma(p) > 0$, and without loss of generality, $|\pi(p)| = 1$. By the Brouwer theorem π has a fixed point, which contradicts 18.17.1.

CHAPTER 19

Nash equilibrium of games and abstract economies

19.0 Remarks and Definitions

A game is a situation in which several players each have partial control over some outcome and generally have conflicting preferences over the outcome. The set of choices under player i's control is denoted X_i. Elements of X_i are called *strategies* and X_i is i's *strategy set*. Letting $N = \{1,...,n\}$ denote the set of players, $X = \prod_{i \in N} X_i$ is the set of strategy vectors. Each strategy vector determines an outcome (which may be a lottery in some models). Players have preferences over outcomes and this induces preferences over strategy vectors. For convenience we will work with preferences over strategy vectors. There ar two ways we might do this. The first is to describe player i's preferences by a binary relation $\tilde{U}_i$ defined on X. Then $\tilde{U}_i(x)$ is the set of all strategy vectors preferred to x. Since player i only has control over the ith component of x, we will find it more useful to describe player i's preferences in terms of the good reply set. Given a strategy vector $x \in X$ and a strategy $y^i \in X_i$, let $x | y_i$ denote the strategy vector obtained from x when player i chooses y_i and the other players keep their choices fixed. Let us say that y_i is a *good reply* for player i to strategy vector x if $x | y_i \in \tilde{U}_i(x)$. This defines a correspondence $U_i : X \twoheadrightarrow X_i$, called the good reply correspondence by $U_i(x) = \{y_i \in X_i : x | y_i \in \tilde{U}_i(x)\}$. It will be convenient to describe preferences in terms of the good reply correspondence U_i rather than the preference relation $\tilde{U}_i$. Note however that we lose some information by doing this. Given a good reply correspondence U_i it will not generally be possible to reconstruct the preference relation $\tilde{U}_i$, unless we know that $\tilde{U}_i$ is transitive, and we will not make this assumption. Thus a *game in strategic form* is a tuple $(N, (X_i), (U_i))$ where each $U_i : \prod_{j \in N} X_j \twoheadrightarrow X_i$.

A shortcoming of this model of a game is that frequently there are situations in which the choices of players cannot be made independently. A simplified example is the pumping of oil out of a common oil field by several producers. Each producer chooses an amount x_i to pump out and sell. The price depends on the total amount sold. Thus each producer has partial control of the price and hence of their profits. But the x_i cannot be chosen independently because their sum cannot exceed the total amount of oil in the ground. To take such possibilities into account we introduce a correspondence $F_i : X \twoheadrightarrow X_i$ which tells which strategies are actually feasible for player i, given the strategy vector of the others. (We have written F_i as a function of the strategies of all the players including i as a technical convenience. In modeling most situations, F_i will be independent of player i's choice.) The jointly feasible strategy vectors are thus the fixed points of the correspondence $F = \prod_{i \in N} F_i : X \twoheadrightarrow X$. A game with the added feasibility or constraint correspondence is called a *generalized game* or *abstract economy*. It is specified by a tuple $(N, (X_i), (F_i), (U_i))$ where $F_i : X \twoheadrightarrow X_i$ and $U_i : X \twoheadrightarrow X_i$.

A *Nash equilibrium* of a strategic form game or abstract economy is a strategy vector x for which no player has a good reply. For a game an equilibrium is an $x \in X$ such that $U_i(x) = \varnothing$ for each i. For an abstract economy an equilibrium is an $x \in X$ such that $x \in F(x)$ and $U_i(x) \cap F_i(x) = \varnothing$ for each i.

Nash [1950] proves the existence of equilibria for games where the players' preferences are representable by continuous quasi-concave utilities and the strategy sets are simplexes. Debreu [1952] proves the existence of equilibrium for abstract economics. He assumes that strategy sets are contractible polyhedra (15.8) and that the feasibility correspondences have closed graph and the maximized utility is continuous and that the set of utility maximizers over each constraint set is contractible. These assumptions are joint assumptions on utility and feasibility and the simplest way to make separate assumptions is to assume that strategy sets are compact and convex and that utilities are continuous and quasi-concave and that the constraint correspondences are continuous with compact convex values. Then the maximum theorem (12.1) guarantees continuity of maximized utility and convexity of the feasible sets and quasi-concavity imply convexity (and hence contractibility) of the set of maximizers. Arrow and Debreu [1954] used Debreu's result to prove the existence of Walrasian equilibrium of an economy and coined the term abstract economy.

Gale and Mas-Colell [1975] prove a lemma which allows them to prove the existence of equilibrium for a game without ordered preferences. They assume that strategy sets are compact convex sets and that the good reply correspondences are convex valued and have open graph. Shafer and Sonnenschein [1975] prove the existence of equilibria for abstract economies without ordered preferences. They assume that the good reply correspondences have open graph and satisfy the convexity/irreflexivity condition $x_i \notin co\ U_i(x)$. They also assume that the feasibility correspondences are continuous with compact convex values. This result does not strictly generalize Debreu's result since convexity rather than contractibility assumptions are made.

19.1 Theorem (cf. Gale and Mas-Colell [1975]; 16.5)
Let $X = \prod_{i \in N} X_i$, X_i being a nonempty, compact, convex subset of $\mathbf{R}^{k_i}$, and let $U_i : X \twoheadrightarrow X_i$ be a correspondence satisfying

(i) $U_i(x)$ is convex for all $x \in X$.
(ii) $U_i^{-}(\{x_i\})$ is open in X for all $x_i \in X_i$.

Then there exists $x \in X$ such that for each i, either $x_i \in U_i(x)$ or $U_i(x) = \varnothing$.

19.2 Proof
Let $W_i = \{x : U_i(x) \neq \varnothing\}$. Then W_i is open by (ii) and $U_i|_{W_i} : W_i \twoheadrightarrow X_i$ satisfies the hypotheses of the selection theorem 14.3, so there is a continuous function $f_i : W_i \rightarrow X_i$ with $f_i(x) \in U_i(x)$. Define the correspondence $\gamma_i : X \twoheadrightarrow X_i$ via

$$\gamma_i(x) = \begin{cases} \{f(x)\} & x \in W_i \\ X_i & \text{otherwise.} \end{cases}$$

Then γ_i is upper hemi-continuous with nonempty compact and convex values, and thus so is $\gamma = \prod_{i \in N} \gamma_i : X \twoheadrightarrow X$. Thus by the Kakutani theorem (15.3), γ has a fixed point $\bar{x}$. If $\gamma_i(\bar{x}) \neq X_i$, then $\bar{x}_i \in \gamma_i(\bar{x})$ implies $x_i = f_i(\bar{x}) \in U_i(\bar{x})$. If $\gamma_i(\bar{x}) = X_i$, then it must be that $U_i(\bar{x}) = \varnothing$. (Unless of course X_i is a singleton, in which case $\{\bar{x}_i\} = \gamma_i(\bar{x})$.)

19.3 Remark
Theorem 19.1 possesses a trivial extension. Each U_i is assumed to satisfy (i) and (ii) so that the selection theorem may be employed. If some U_i is already a singleton-valued correspondence, then the selection problem is trivial. Thus we may allow some of the U_i's to be continuous singleton-valued correspondences instead, and the conclusion follows. Corollary 19.4 is derived from 19.1 by assuming each $x_i \notin U_i(x)$ and concludes that there exists some x such that $U_i(x) = \varnothing$ for each i. Assuming that $U_i(x)$ is never empty yields a result equivalent to 16.5.

19.4 Corollary
For each i, let $U_i : X \twoheadrightarrow X_i$ have open graph and satisfy $x_i \notin co\ U_i(x)$ for each x. Then there exists $x \in X$ with $U_i(x) = \varnothing$ for all i.

19.5 Proof

By 11.29 the correspondences $co\ U_i$ satisfy the hypotheses of 19.1 so there is $x \in X$ such that for each i, $x_i \in co\ U_i(x)$ or $co\ U_i(x) = \emptyset$. Since $x_i \notin co\ U_i(x)$ by hypothesis, we have $co\ U_i(x) = \emptyset$, so $U_i(x) = \emptyset$.

19.6 Remark

Corollary 19.4 can be derived from Theorem 7.2 by reducing the multi-player game to a 1-person game. The technique described below is due to Borglin and Keiding [1976].

19.7 Alternate Proof of Corollary 19.4 (Borglin and Keiding [1976])

For each i, define $\tilde{U}_i : X \twoheadrightarrow X$ by

$$\tilde{U}_i(x) = X_1 \times \cdots \times X_{i-1} \times U_i(x) \times X_{i+1} \times \cdots \times X_n.$$

Set $I(x) = \{i : \tilde{U}_i(x) \neq \emptyset\}$ and let

$$P(x) = \begin{cases} \bigcap_{i \in I(x)} \tilde{U}_i(x) & \text{if } I(x) \neq \emptyset \\ \emptyset & \text{otherwise.} \end{cases}$$

Now each $\tilde{U}_i$ is FS and P is locally majorized by some $\tilde{U}_i$ everywhere. Thus by 7.19, there is an $\bar{x}$ with $P(x) = \emptyset$. It then follows that $U_i(\bar{x}) = \emptyset$ for all i.

19.8 Theorem (Shafer and Sonnenschein [1975])

Let $(N, (X_i), (F_i), (U_i))$ be an abstract economy such that for each i,

(i) $X_i \subset \mathbf{R}^{k_i}$ is nonempty, compact and convex.

(ii) F_i is a continuous correspondence with nonempty compact convex values.

(iii) $Gr\ U_i$ is open in $X \times X_i$.

(iv) $x_i \notin co\ U_i(x)$ for all $x \in X$.

Then there is an equilibrium.

19.9 Proof (Shafer and Sonnenschein [1975])

Define $v_i : X \times X_i \to \mathbf{R}_+$ by $v_i(x,y_i) = dist\ [(x,y_i), (Gr\ U_i)^c]$. Then $v_i(x,y_i) > 0$ if and only if $y_i \in U_i(x)$ and v_i is continuous since $Gr\ U_i$ is open (2.7). Define $H_i : X \twoheadrightarrow X_i$ via

$$H_i(x) = \{y_i \in X_i : y_i \text{ maximizes } v_i(x,\cdot) \text{ on } F_i(x)\}.$$

Then H_i has nonempty compact values and is upper hemi-continuous and hence closed. (To see that H_i is upper hemi-continuous, apply the maximum theorem (12.1) to the correspondence

$(x,y_i) \mapsto\!\!\!\to \{x\} \times F_i(x)$ and the function v_i.) Define $G : X \to\!\!\!\to X$ via $G(x) = \prod_{i=1}^{N} co\ H_i(x)$. Then by 11.25 and 11.29, G is upper hemi-continuous with compact convex values and so satisfies the hypotheses of the Kakutani fixed point theorem, so there is $\bar{x} \in X$ with $\bar{x} \in G(\bar{x})$. Since $H_i(\bar{x}) \subset F_i(\bar{x})$ which is convex, $\bar{x}_i \in G_i(\bar{x}) = co\ H_i(\bar{x}) \subset F_i(\bar{x})$. We now show $U_i(\bar{x}) \cap F_i(\bar{x}) = \varnothing$. Suppose not; i.e., suppose there is $z_i \in U_i(\bar{x}) \cap F_i(\bar{x})$. Then since $z_i \in U_i(\bar{x})$ we have $v_i(\bar{x},z_i) > 0$, and since $H_i(\bar{x})$ consists of the maximizers of $v_i(\bar{x},\cdot)$ on $F_i(\bar{x})$, we have that $v_i(\bar{x},y_i) > 0$ for all $y_i \in H_i(\bar{x})$. This says that $y_i \in U_i(\bar{x})$ for all $y_i \in H_i(\bar{x})$. Thus $H_i(\bar{x}) \subset U_i(\bar{x})$, so $\bar{x}_i \in G_i(\bar{x}) = co\ H_i(\bar{x}) \subset co\ U_i(\bar{x})$, which contradicts (iv). Thus $U_i(\bar{x}) \cap F_i(\bar{x}) = \varnothing$.

19.10 Remark

The correspondences H_i used in the proof of Theorem 19.8 are not natural constructions, which is the cleverness of Shafer and Sonnenschein's proof. The natural approach would be to use the best reply correspondences, $x \mapsto\!\!\!\to \{x_i : U_i(x|x_i) \cap F_i(x) = \varnothing\}$. By Theorem 12.3, these correspondences are compact-valued and upper hemi-continuous. They may fail to be convex-valued, however. Mas-Colell [1974] gives an example for which the best reply correspondence has no connected-valued subcorrespondence. Taking the convex hull of the best reply correspondence does not help, since a fixed point of the convex hull correspondence may fail to be an equilibrium.

Another natural approach would be to use the good reply correspondence $x \mapsto\!\!\!\to co\ U_i(x) \cap F_i(x)$. This correspondence, while convex-valued, is not closed-valued, and so the Kakutani theorem does not apply. What Shafer and Sonnenschein do is choose a correspondence that is a subcorrespondence of the good reply set when it is nonempty and equal to the whole feasible strategy set otherwise. Under stronger assumptions on the F_i correspondences this approach can be made to work without taking a proper subset of the good reply set. The additional assumptions on F_i are the following. First, $F_i(x)$ is assumed to be topologically regular for each x, i.e., $F_i(x) = cl\ [int\ F_i(x)]$. Second, the correspondence $x \mapsto\!\!\!\to int\ F_i(x)$ is assumed to have open graph. The requirement of open graph is stronger than lower hemi-continuity. These assumptions were used by Borglin and Keiding [1976] who reduced the multi-player abstract economy to a 1-person game. The proof below adds an additional player to the abstract economy by introducing an "abstract auctioneer," and incorporates the feasibility constraints into the preferences which converts it into a game. Both the topological regularity and open graph assumptions are satisfied by budget correspondences, provided income is always greater than the minimum consumption expenditures on the consumption set. The proof is closely related to the arguments used by Gale and Mas-Colell [1975] to reduce an economy to a noncooperative game.

19.11 A Special Case of Theorem 19.8

Let $(N, (X_i), (F_i), (U_i))$ be an abstract economy such that for each i,

(i) $X_i \subset \mathbf{R}^{k_i}$ is nonempty, compact and convex.

(ii) F_i is an upper hemi-continuous correspondence with nonempty compact convex values satisfying, for all x, $F_i(x) = cl\ [int\ F_i(x)]$ and $x \mapsto\!\!\rightarrow int\ F_i(x)$ has open graph.

(iii) $\mathrm{Gr}\ U_i$ is open in $X \times X_i$.

(iv) for all x, $x_i \notin co\ U_i(x)$.

Then there is an equilibrium, i.e., an $\bar{x} \in X$ such that for each i,

$$\bar{x}_i \in F_i(\bar{x})$$

and

$$U_i(\bar{x}) \cap F_i(\bar{x}) = \varnothing.$$

19.12 19.12 Proof

We define a game as follows.

Put $Z_0 = \prod_{i \in N} X_i$. For $i \in N$ put $Z_i = X_i$, and set $Z = Z_0 \times \prod_{i \in N} Z_i$. A typical element of Z will be denoted (x,y), where $x \in Z_0$ and $y \in \prod_{i \in N} Z_i$. Define preference correspondences $\mu_i : Z \rightarrow\!\!\rightarrow Z_i$ as follows.

Define μ_0 by

$$\mu_0(x,y) = \{y\},$$

and for $i \in N$ set

$$\mu_i(x,y) = \begin{cases} int\ F_i(x) & \text{if } y_i \notin F_i(x) \\ co\ U_i(y) \cap int\ F_i(x) & \text{if } y_i \in F_i(x). \end{cases}$$

Note that μ_0 is continuous and never empty-valued and that for $i \in N$ the correspondence μ_i is convex-valued and satisfies $y_i \notin \mu_i(x,y)$. Also for $i \in N$, the graph of μ_i is open. To see this set

$$A_i = \{(x,y,z_i) : z_i \in int\ F_i(x)\},$$

$$B_i = \{(x,y,z_i) : y_i \notin F_i(x)\},$$

$$C_i = \{(x,y,z_i) : z_i \in co\ U_i(y)\},$$

and note that

$$Gr\ \mu_i = (A_i \cap B_i) \cup (A_i \cap C_i).$$

The set A_i is open because *int* F_i has open graph and C_i is open by hypothesis (iii). The set B_i is also open: If $y_i \notin F_i(x)$, then there is a closed neighborhood W of y_i such that $F_i(x) \subset W^c$, and upper hemi-continuity of F_i then gives the desired result.

Thus the hypothesis of Remark 19.3 is satisfied and so there exists $(\bar{x},\bar{y}) \in Z$ such that

$$\bar{x} \in \mu_0(\bar{x},\bar{y}) \qquad 19.13$$

and for $i \in N$

$$\mu_i(\bar{x},\bar{y}) = \varnothing. \qquad 19.14$$

Now (19.13) implies $\bar{x} = \bar{y}$; and since $F_i(x)$ is never empty, 19.14 becomes

$$co\ U_i(\bar{x}) \cap int\ F_i(\bar{x}) = \varnothing \quad \text{for } i \in N.$$

Thus $U_i(\bar{x}) \cap int\ F_i(\bar{x}) = \varnothing$. But $F_i(\bar{x}) = cl\ [int\ F_i(\bar{x})]$ and $U_i(\bar{x})$ is open, so $U_i(\bar{x}) \cap F_i(\bar{x}) = \varnothing$; i.e., $\bar{x}$ is an equilibrium.

CHAPTER 20

Walrasian equilibrium of an economy

20.0 Remarks

We now have several tools at our disposal for proving the existence of a Walrasian equilibrium of an economy. There are many ways open to do this. We will focus on two approaches. Other approaches will be described and references given at the end of this chapter. The two approaches are the excess demand approach and the abstract economy approach. The excess demand approach utilizes the Debreu-Gale-Nikaido lemma (18.1). The abstract economy approach converts the problem of finding a Walrasian equilibrium of the economy into the problem of finding the Nash equilibrium of an associated abstract economy.

The central difficulty of the excess demand approach involves proving the upper hemi-continuity of the excess demand correspondence. The maximum theorem (12.1) is used to accomplish this, but the problem that must be overcome is the failure of the budget correspondence to be lower hemi-continuous when a consumer's income is at the minimum compatible with his consumption set (cf. 11.18(e)). When this occurs, the maximum theorem can no longer be used to guarantee the upper hemi-continuity of the consumer's demand correspondence. There are two ways to deal with this problem. The first is to assume it away, by assuming each consumer has an endowment large enough to provide him with more than his minimum income for any relevant price vector. The other approach is to patch up the demand correspondence's discontinuities at places where the income reaches its minimum or less, then add some sort of interrelatedness assumption on the consumers to guarantee that in equilibrium, they will all have sufficient income. This latter approach is clearly preferable, but is much more complicated than the first approach. In the interest of simplicity, we will make use of the first approach and provide references to other approaches at the end of the chapter.

The abstract economy approach explicitly introduces a fictitious agent, the "auctioneer," into the picture and models the economy as an abstract economy or generalized game. The strategies of consumers are consumption vectors, the strategies of suppliers are production vectors, and the strategies of the auctioneer are prices. The auctioneer's preferences are to increase the value of excess demand. A Nash equilibrium of the abstract economy corresponds to a Walrasian equilibrium of the original economy. The principal difficulty to overcome in applying the existence theorems for abstract economies is the fact that they require compact strategy sets and the consumption and production sets are not compact. This problem is dealt with by showing that any equilibrium must lie in a compact set, then truncating the consumption and production sets and showing that the Nash equilibrium of the truncated abstract economy is a Walrasian equilibrium of the original economy.

20.1 Notation

Let $\mathbf{R}^m$ denote the commodity space. For $i = 1,...,n$ let $X_i \subset \mathbf{R}^m$ denote the ith consumer's consumption set, $w_i \in \mathbf{R}^n$ his private endowment, and U_i his preference relation on X_i. For $j = i,...,k$ let Y_j denote the jth supplier's production set. Set $X = \sum_{i=1}^{n} X_i$, $w = \sum_{i=1}^{n} w_i$ and $Y = \sum_{j=1}^{k} Y_j$. Let α_j^i denote the share of consumer i in the profits of supplier j. An economy is then described by a tuple $((X_i,w_i,U_i), (Y_j), (\alpha_j^i))$.

20.2 Definitions

An *attainable state* of the economy is a tuple $((x_i),(y_j)) \in \prod_{i=1}^{n} X_i \times \prod_{j=1}^{k} Y_j$, satisfying

$$\sum_{i=1}^{n} x_i - \sum_{j=1}^{k} y_j - w = 0.$$

Let F denote the set of attainable states and let

$$M = \{((x_i),(y_j)) \in (\mathbf{R}^m)^{n+k} : \sum_{i=l}^{n} X_i - \sum_{j=1}^{n} Y_j - w = 0\}.$$

Then $F = (\Pi X_i \times \Pi Y_j) \cap M$. Let $\tilde{X}_i$ be the projection of F on X_i, and let $\tilde{Y}_j$ be the projection of F on Y_j.

A *Walrasian free disposal equilibrium* is a price $p^* \in \Delta$ together with an attainable state $((x_i^*),(y_j^*))$ satisfying:

(i) For each $j = 1,...,k$,

$$p^* \cdot y_j^* \geqslant p^* \cdot y_j \text{ for all } y_j \in Y_j.$$

(ii) For each $i = 1,...,n$,

$$x_i^* \in B_i \text{ and } U_i(x_i^*) \cap B_i = \varnothing,$$

where

$$B_i = \{x_i \in X_i : p^* \cdot x_i \leqslant p^* \cdot w_i + \sum_{j=1}^{k} \alpha_j^i(p^* \cdot y_j^*)\}.$$

20.3 Proposition

Let the economy $((X_i,w_i,U_i), (Y_j), (\alpha_j^i))$ satisfy:
For each $i = 1,...,n$,
20.3.1 X_i is closed, convex and bounded from below; and $w_i \in X_i$.
For each $j = 1,...,k$ that
20.3.2 Y_j is closed, convex and $0 \in Y_j$.
20.3.3 $\mathbf{A}Y \cap \mathbf{R}_+^n = \{0\}$.
20.3.4 $Y \cap -Y = \{0\}$.

Then the set F of attainable states is compact and nonempty. Furthermore, $0 \in \tilde{Y}_j$, $j = 1,...,k$.

Suppose in addition, that the following two assumptions hold. For each $i = 1,...,n$,
20.3.5 there is some $\bar{x}_i \in X_i$ satisfying $w_i > \bar{x}_i$.
20.3.6 $Y \supset -\mathbf{R}_+^m$.

Then $\bar{x}_i \in \tilde{X}_i$, $i = 1,...,n$.

20.4 Proof (cf. Debreu [1959, p. 77-78])

Clearly $((w_i), (0_j)) \in F$, so F is nonempty and $0 \in \tilde{Y}_j$. The set F of attainable states is clearly closed, being the intersection of two closed sets, so by Proposition 2.36, it suffices to show that $\mathbf{A}F = \{0\}$. By Exercise 2.35,

$$\mathbf{A}F \subset \mathbf{A}(\prod_{i=1}^{n} X_i \times \prod_{j=1}^{k} Y_j) \cap \mathbf{A}M.$$

Also by 2.35, $\mathbf{A}(\prod_{i=1}^{n} X_i \times \prod_{j=1}^{k} Y_j) \subset \prod_{i=1}^{n} \mathbf{A}X_i \times \prod_{j=1}^{k} \mathbf{A}Y_j$. Since each X_i is bounded below there is some $b_i \in \mathbf{R}^m$ such that $X_i \subset b_i + \mathbf{R}_+^m$. Thus $\mathbf{A}X_i \subset \mathbf{A}(b_i + \mathbf{R}_+^m) = \mathbf{A}\mathbf{R}_+^m = \mathbf{R}_+^m$. Also by 2.35, $\mathbf{A}Y_j \subset \mathbf{A}Y$. Again by 2.35, since $M-w$ is a cone, $\mathbf{A}M = M-w$. Thus we can show $\mathbf{A}F = \{0\}$ if we can show that

$$(\prod_{i=1}^{n} \mathbf{R}_+^m \times \Pi_{j=1}^{k} \mathbf{A}Y) \cap (M-w) = \{0\}.$$

In other words, we need to show that if $x_i \in \mathbf{R}_+^m$, $i = 1,...,n$, and $y_j \in \mathbf{A}Y$, $j = 1,...,k$ and $\sum_{i=1}^{n} x_i - \sum_{j=1}^{k} y_j = 0$, then

$x_1 = \ldots x_n = y_1 \ldots = y_k = 0$. Now $\sum_{i=1}^{n} x_i \geqslant 0$, so that $\sum_{j=1}^{k} y_j \geqslant 0$ too. Since $\mathbf{A}Y$ is a convex cone (2.35), $\sum_{j=1}^{k} y_j \in \mathbf{A}Y$. Since $\mathbf{A}Y \cap \mathbf{R}_+^m = \{0\}$, $\sum_{i=1}^{n} x_i - \sum_{j=1}^{k} y_j = 0$ implies $\sum_{i=1}^{n} x_i = 0 = \sum_{j=1}^{k} y_j$. Now $x_i \geqslant 0$ and $\sum_{i=1}^{n} x_i = 0$ clearly imply that $x_i = 0$, $i = 1,\ldots,n$. Rewriting $\sum_{j=1}^{k} y_j = 0$ yields $y_i = -(\sum_{j \neq i} y_j)$. Both y_i and this last sum belong to Y as $\mathbf{A}Y \subset Y$ (again by 2.35). Thus $y_i \in Y \cap (-Y)$ so $y_i = 0$. This is true for all $i = 1,\ldots,k$.

Now assume that 20.3.5 and 20.3.6 hold. By 20.3.5, $\sum_{i=1}^{n} \bar{x}_i < \sum_{i=1}^{n} w_i$. Set $\bar{y} = \sum_{i=1}^{n} \bar{x}_i - \sum_{i=1}^{n} w_i$. Then $y < 0$, so by 20.3.6 there are $\bar{y}_j$, $j = 1,\ldots,k$, satisfying $\bar{y} = \sum_{j=1}^{k} \bar{y}_j$. Then $((\bar{x}_i),(\bar{y}_j)) \in F$, so $\bar{x}_i \in \tilde{X}_i$.

20.5 Notation

Under the hypotheses of Proposition 20.3 the set F of attainable states is compact. Thus for each consumer i, there is a compact convex set K_i containing $\tilde{X}_i$ in its interior. Set $X_i' = K_i \cap X_i$. Then $\tilde{X}_i \subset int\ X_i'$. Likewise, for each supplier j there is a compact convex set C_j containing $\tilde{Y}_j$ in its interior. Set $Y_j' = C_j \cap Y_j$.

20.6 Theorem

Let the economy $((X_i,w_i,U_i), (Y_j), (\alpha_j^i))$ satisfy:

For each $i = 1,\ldots,n$,

20.6.1 X_i is closed, convex, bounded from below, and $w_i \in X_i$.

20.6.2 There is some $\bar{x}_i \in X_i$ satisfying $w_i > \bar{x}_i$.

20.6.3 (a) U_i has open graph,

(b) $x_i \notin co\ U_i(x_i)$,

(c) $x_i \in cl\ U_i(x_i)$.

For each $j = 1,\ldots,k$,

20.6.4 Y_j is closed and convex and $0 \in Y_j$.

20.6.5 $Y \cap \mathbf{R}_+^m = \{0\}$.

20.6.6 $Y \cap (-Y) = \{0\}$.

20.6.7 $Y \supset -\mathbf{R}_+^m$.

Then there is a free disposal equilibrium of the economy.

20.7 Proof (cf. Debreu [1959; 1982])
Define an abstract economy as follows. Player 0 is the auctioneer. His strategy set is Δ_{m-1}, the closed standard $(m-1)$-simplex. These strategies will be price vectors. The strategy set of consumer i will be X_i'. The strategy set of supplier j is Y_j'. A typical strategy vector is thus of the form $(p,(x_i),(y_j))$.

The auctioneer's preferences are represented by the correspondence $U_0 : \Delta \times \prod_i X_i' \times \prod_j Y_j' \twoheadrightarrow \Delta$ defined by

$$U_0(p,(x_i),(y_j)) = \{q \in \Delta : q \cdot (\sum_i x_i - \sum_j y_j - w) > p \cdot (\sum_i x_i - \sum_j y_j - w)\}.$$

Thus the auctioneer prefers to raise the value of excess demand. Observe that U_0 has open graph, convex upper contour sets and $p \notin U_0(p,(x_i),(y_j))$.

Supplier j^*'s preferences are represented by the correspondence $V_{j^*} : \Delta \times \prod_i X_i' \times \prod_j Y_j' \twoheadrightarrow Y_{j^*}'$ defined by

$$V_{j^*}(p,(x_i),(y_j)) = \{y_{j^*}' \in Y_{j^*}' : p \cdot y_{j^*}' > p \cdot y_{j^*}\}.$$

Thus suppliers prefer larger profits. These correspondences have open graph, convex upper contour sets and satisfy $y_{j^*} \notin V_{j^*}(p,(x_i),(y_j))$.

The preferences of consumer i^* are represented by the correspondence $\tilde{U}_{i^*} : \Delta \times \prod_i X_i' \times \prod_j Y_j'$ defined by

$$\tilde{U}_{i^*}(p,(x_i),(y_j)) = co\ U_{i^*}(x_{i^*}).$$

This correspondence has open graph by 11.29(c), convex upper contour sets and satisfies $x_i^* \notin U_{i^*}(p,(x_i),(y_j))$.

The feasibility correspondences are as follows. For suppliers and the auctioneer, they are constant correspondences and the values are equal to their entire strategy sets. Thus they are continuous with compact convex values. For consumers things are more complicated. Start by setting $\pi_j(p) = \max_{y_j \in Y_j} p \cdot y_j$. By the maximum theorem (13.1) this is a continuous function. Since $0 \in \tilde{Y}_j$, $\pi_j(p)$ is always nonnegative. Set

$$F_{i^*}(p,(x_i),(y_j)) = \left\{x_{i^*}' \in X_{i^*}' : p \cdot x_{i^*}' \leqslant p \cdot w_{i^*} = \sum_{j=1}^{k} \alpha_j^{i^*} \pi_j(p)\right\}.$$

Since $\pi_j(p)$ is nonnegative and $\bar{x}_{i^*} < w_i$ in X_i', $p \cdot \bar{x}_i < p \cdot w_i$ for any $p \in \Delta$. Thus F_{i^*} is lower hemi-continuous (11.18(e)) and nonempty-valued. Since X'_{i*} is compact, F_{i*} is upper hemi-continuous, since it clearly has closed graph. Thus for each consumer, the feasibility correspondence is a continuous correspondence with nonempty compact convex values.

The abstract economy so constructed satisfies all the hypotheses of the Shafer-Sonnenschein theorem (19.8) and so has a Nash equilibrium. Translating the definition of Nash equilibrium to the case at hand yields the existence of $(p^*,(x_i^*),(\bar{y}_j)) \in \Delta \times \prod_i X'_i \times \prod_j Y'_j$ satisfying

(i) $q \cdot (\sum_i x_i^* - \sum_j \bar{y}_j - w) \leqslant p^* \cdot (\sum_i x_i^* - \sum_j \bar{y}_j - w)$ for all $q \in \Delta$.

(ii) $p^* \cdot \bar{y}_j \geqslant p^* \cdot y_j$ for all $y_j \in Y'_j$, $j = 1,...,k$.

(iii) $x_i^* \in B_i$ and $co\ U_i(x_i^*) \cap B_i = \varnothing$, $i = 1,...,n$, where
$$B_i = \{x_i \in X'_i : p^* \cdot x_i \leqslant p^* \cdot w_i + \sum_{j=1}^{k} \alpha_i^j (p^* \cdot \bar{y}_j)\}.$$

Let $M_i = p^* \cdot w_i + \sum_{j=1}^{k} \alpha_i^j (p^* \cdot \bar{y}_j)$. Then in fact, each consumer spends all his income, so that we have the budget equality $p^* \cdot x_i^* = M_i$. Suppose not. Then since $U_i(x_i^*)$ is open and $x_i^* \in cl\ U_i(x_i^*)$, it would follow that $U_i(x_i^*) \cap B_i \neq \varnothing$, a contradiction.

Summing up the budget equalities and using $\sum_i \alpha_i^j = 1$ for each j yields $p^* \cdot \sum_i x_i^* = p^*(\sum_j \bar{y}_j + w)$, so that
$$p^* \cdot (\sum_i x_i^* - \sum_j \bar{y}_j - w) = 0.$$

This and (i) yield
$$\sum_{i=1}^{n} x_i^* - \sum_j \bar{y}_j - w \leqslant 0.$$

We next show that $p^* \cdot \bar{y}_j \geqslant p^* \cdot y_j$ for all $y_j \in Y_j$. Suppose not, and let $p^* \cdot y'_j > p^* \cdot \bar{y}_j$. Since Y_j is convex, $\lambda y'_j + (1 - \lambda)\bar{y}_j \in Y_j$, and it too yields a higher profit than $\bar{y}_j$. But for λ small enough, $\lambda y'_j + (1 - \lambda)\bar{y}_j \in Y'_j$, because $\tilde{Y}_j$ is in the interior of C_j (20.5). This contradicts (ii).

By 20.6.7, $z^* = \sum_{i=1}^{n} x_i^* - \sum_j \bar{y}_j - w \ \in Y$, so that there exist $y'_j \in Y_j$, $j = 1,...,n$ satisfying $z^* = \sum_j y'_j$. Set $y_j^* = \bar{y}_j + y'_j$. Since each $\bar{y}_j$ maximizes $p^* \cdot y_j$ over Y_j, then $\sum_j \bar{y}_j$ maximizes $p^* \cdot y$ over Y. But since $p^* \cdot z^* = 0$, $\sum_j y_j^*$ also maximizes p^* over Y. But then each y_j^* must also maximize $p^* \cdot y_j$ over Y_j. Thus we have so far shown that $p^* \cdot y_j^* \geqslant p^* \cdot y_j$ for all $y_j \in Y_j$, $j = 1,...,n$. By construction, we have that $((x_i^*),(y_j^*)) \in F$. To show that $(p^*,(x_i^*),(y_j^*))$ is indeed a Walrasian free disposal equilibrium it remains to be proven that for each i,

$$U_i(x_i^*) \cap \{x_i \in X_i : p^* \cdot x_i \leqslant p^* \cdot w_i + \sum_j \alpha_j^i (p^* \cdot y_j^*)\} = \varnothing.$$

Suppose that there is some x_i' belonging to this intersection. Then for small enough $\lambda > 0$, $\lambda x_i' + (1 - \lambda)x_i^* \in X_i'$ and since $x_i^* \in cl\ U_i(x_i^*)$, $\lambda x_i' + (1 - \lambda)x_i^* \in co\ U_i(x_i^*) \cap B_i$, contradicting (iii). Thus $((x_i^*),(y_j^*))$ is a Walrasian free disposal equilibrium.

20.8 Remarks

In order to use the excess demand approach, stronger hypotheses will be used. Mas-Colell [1974] gives an example which shows that under the hypotheses made on preferences in Theorem 20.6, consumer demand correspondences need not be convex-valued or even have an upper hemi-continuous selection with connected values. Since the Gale-Debreu-Nikaido lemma (18.1) requires a convex-valued excess demand correspondence, it cannot be directly used to prove existence of equilibrium. By strengthening the hypotheses on preferences so that there is a continuous quasi-concave utility representing them we get upper hemi-continuous convex-valued demand correspondences.

20.9 Theorem

Let the economy $((X_i,w_i,U_i),(Y_j),(\alpha_j^i))$ satisfy the hypotheses of Theorem 20.6 and further assume that there is a continuous quasi-concave utility u_i satisfying $U_i(x_i) = \{x_i' \in X_i : u_i(x_i' > u_i(x_i)\}$.

Then the economy has a Walrasian free disposal equilibrium.

20.10 Proof

Let Y_j' be as in 20.5 and define $\gamma_j : \Delta \twoheadrightarrow Y_j'$ by

$$\gamma_j(p) = \{y_j \in Y_j' : p \cdot y_j \geqslant p \cdot y_j' \text{ for all } y_j' \in Y_j'\}.$$

Define $\pi_j(p) = \max_{y_j \in Y_j'} p \cdot y_j$. By the maximum theorem (12.1), γ_j is upper hemi-continuous with nonempty compact values and π_j is continuous. Since $0 \in Y_j$, π_j is nonnegative. Since Y_j' is convex, $\gamma_j(p)$ is convex too.

Let X_i' be as in 20.5 and define $\beta_i : \Delta \twoheadrightarrow X_i'$ by

$$\beta_i(p) = \{x_i \in X_i' : p \cdot x_i \leqslant p \cdot w_i + \sum_j \alpha_j^i \pi_j(p)\}.$$

As in 20.7 the existence of $\bar{x}_i < w_i$ in X_i' implies that β_i is a continuous correspondence with nonempty values. Since X_i' is compact and convex, β_i has compact convex values. Define $\mu_i : \Delta \twoheadrightarrow X_i'$ by

$$\mu_i(p) = \{x_i \in \beta_i(p) : u_i(x_i) \geqslant u_i(x_i') \text{ for all } x_i' \in \beta_i(p)\}.$$

By 12.1, μ_i is an upper hemi-continuous correspondence with nonempty compact values. Since u_i is quasi-concave, μ_i has convex values. Set

$$Z(p) = \sum_{i=1}^{n} \mu_i(p) - \sum_{j=1}^{k} \gamma_i(p) - w.$$

By 11.27, Z is upper hemi-continuous and by 2.43 has nonempty compact convex values. Also for any $z \in Z(p)$, $p \cdot z \leqslant 0$. To see this just add up the budget correspondences for each consumer.

By 18.1, there is some $p^* \in \Delta$ and $z^* \in Z(p^*)$ satisfying $z^* \leqslant 0$. Thus there are $x_i^* \in \mu_i(p^*)$ and $y_j^* \in \gamma_j(p^*)$ such that

$$\sum_i x_i^* - \sum_j y_j^* - w \leqslant 0.$$

It follows just as in 20.7 that $((x_i^*),(y_j^*))$ is a Walrasian free disposal equilibrium.

20.11 Remarks

The literature on Walrasian equilibrium is enormous. Two standard texts in the field are Debreu [1959] and Arrow and Hahn [1971]. There are excellent recent surveys by Debreu [1982], McKenzie [1981] and Sonnenschein [1977]. The theorems presented here are quite crude compared to the state of the art. They were included primarily to show that there is much more to proving the existence of a Walrasian equilibrium under reasonable hypotheses than a simple invoking of a clever fixed point argument. The assumptions used can be weakened in several directions. The following is only a partial list, and no attempt has been made to completely document the literature.

Assumption 20.6.2, which says that every consumer can get by with less of every commodity than he is endowed with, is excessively strong. It has been weakened by Debreu [1962] and in a more significant way by Moore [1975]. Assumption 20.6.6 says that production is irreversible. This assumption was dispensed with by McKenzie [1959; 1961]. A coordinate-free version of some of the assumptions was given by Debreu [1962], without referring to $\mathbf{R}_+^m$ or lower bounds. It is not really necessary to assume that each individual production set is closed and convex (Debreu [1959]). McKenzie [1955] allowed for interdependencies among consumers in their preferences, as do Shafer and Sonnenschein [1976]. The assumption of free disposability of commodities (20.6.7) was dropped by McKenzie [1955] and has received a lot of attention recently in papers by Bergstrom [1976], Hart and Kuhn [1975] and others. McKenzie [1981] adapts the excess demand approach to the case of nonordered preferences. The basic breakthrough in dispensing with ordered preferences are Sonnenschein [1971] and Mas-Colell [1974].

Another approach to proving the existence of Walrasian equilibrium by using fixed point theory is not considered here. It involves finding "efficient" allocations and prices which support them. This sort of technique was used by Negishi [1960], Arrow and Hahn [1971] and Moore [1975].

CHAPTER 21

More interconnections

21.1 Von Neumann's Intersection Lemma (16.4) Implies Kakutani's Theorem (15.3) (Nikaido [1968, p. 70])

Let $\gamma : K \twoheadrightarrow K$ satisfy the hypotheses of 15.3 and set $X = Y = K$, $E = Gr\ \gamma$ and set F equal to the diagonal of $X \times X$. The hypotheses of 16.4 are then satisfied, and $E \cap F$ is equal to the set of fixed points of γ.

21.2 The Fan-Browder Theorem (17.1) Implies Kakutani's Theorem (15.3)

Let $\gamma : K \twoheadrightarrow K$ be convex-valued and closed and let $\mu(x) = \{x\}$ for each x. Then $x \in \gamma(x)$ if and only if $\gamma(x) \cap \mu(x) \neq \varnothing$. Setting $\lambda = 1$, $v = x$ and $y = u \in \gamma(x)$, the hypotheses of 17.1 are satisfied. Thus the set of fixed points of γ is compact and nonempty.

21.3 Remark

In the hypotheses of Theorem 17.1 if $\gamma(x) \cap \mu(x) \neq \varnothing$, then we can take $u = v$ and $y = x$. Thus if we associate to each x the set of y's given by the hypothesis, we are looking for a fixed point of the correspondence. This correspondence cannot be closed-valued however, since λ is required to be strictly positive. Thus we cannot use the Kakutani theorem to prove Theorem 17.1 in this fashion. Note that the proof of Theorem 17.1 depends only on Fan's lemma (7.4), which depends only on the K-K-M lemma (5.4), which can be proved from Sperner's lemma (4.1).

21.4 The Brouwer Theorem (6.1) Implies Fan's Lemma (7.4)

Define $\gamma : X \twoheadrightarrow X$ via $\gamma(y) = \{x \in X : (x,y) \notin E\}$. By (ii), γ is convex-valued and since E is closed, γ has open graph. If $X \times \{y\} \subset E$, then $\gamma(y) = \varnothing$. Suppose $\gamma(y)$ is never empty. Then by the selection theorem (14.3) γ has a continuous selection $f : X \to X$, which has a fixed point, contrary to (i).

21.5 A Proof of Theorem 18.1 Based on Theorem 15.1 (cf. 9.11; Kuhn [1956]; Nikaido [1968, Theorem 16.6])

Recall $\gamma : \Delta \twoheadrightarrow \mathbf{R}^m$ satisfies $p \cdot z \leqslant 0$ for all $z \in \gamma(p)$, where γ is upper hemi-continuous and nonempty and compact and convex-valued, and hence γ is closed. Since Δ is compact and γ is upper hemi-continuous and compact-valued, $\gamma(\Delta)$ is compact, so $F = co\ \gamma(\Delta)$ is compact. We now define the price adjustment function $f : \Delta \times F \to \Delta$ by

$$f(p,z) = \frac{p + z^+}{1 + \sum_i z_i^+},$$

where $z_i^+ = \max\{z_i,0\}$ and $z^+ = (z_0^+, \ldots, z_n^+)$. Intuitively, if $z_i > 0$ then good i is in excess demand so we want to raise p_i, which is what f does. Note that f is continuous and its range is Δ. Define the correspondence $\mu : \Delta \twoheadrightarrow \Delta$ via

$$\mu(p) = \{f(p,z) : z \in \gamma(p)\}.$$

Then by 15.1 μ has a fixed point $\bar{p}$. Thus

$$\bar{p} = \frac{\bar{p} + z^+}{1 + \sum_i z_i^+} \quad \text{for some } z \in \gamma(p).$$

Since $\bar{p} \cdot z \leqslant 0$, for some j we must have $\bar{p}_j > 0$ and $z_j \leqslant 0$. (Otherwise $\bar{p} \cdot z > 0$.) For this j, $z_j^+ = 0$, and since

$$\bar{p} = \frac{\bar{p} + z^+}{1 + \sum_i z_i^+},$$

we must have $\sum_i z_i^+ = 0$. But this implies $z \leqslant 0$.

21.6 Another Proof of Lemma 8.1 (Ichiishi [1983]; cf. 21.7)
Define the correspondence $\gamma : K \twoheadrightarrow K$ via $\gamma(x) = \{y \in K : \text{for all } z \in K, f(x) \cdot y \geqslant f(x) \cdot z\}$. Then γ has nonempty compact convex values and by the maximum theorem (12.1), γ is closed. The fixed points of γ are precisely the points we want, so the conclusion of 8.1 follows from Kakutani's theorem (15.3).

21.7 A Proof of Theorem 18.6 Based on Kakutani's Theorem (15.3) and the Maximum Theorem (12.1) (Debreu [1956]; cf. Nikaido [1956])
By 18.3 there is a homeomorphism $h : K \to D$, where K is compact and convex. Let $Z = co\ (\gamma \circ h)(K)$. Since γ is upper hemi-continuous and compact-valued, it follows from 11.16 that Z is compact. Define $\mu : Z \twoheadrightarrow K$ via

$$\mu(z) = \{p \in K : \text{for all } q \in K, h(p) \cdot z \geqslant h(q) \cdot z\}.$$

It follows from the maximum theorem (12.1) that μ is upper hemi-continuous and compact-valued. (Consider the continuous correspondence $z \mapsto\!\!\to \{z\} \times K$ and the continuous function $(z,p) \mapsto p \cdot z$.) It is easily seen that μ is convex-valued. Thus the correspondence $(p,z) \mapsto\!\!\to \mu(z) \times \gamma(p)$ maps $K \times Z$ into itself and is closed by 11.9, so by the Kakutani theorem (15.3) there are p^* and z^* with $z^* \in \gamma(p^*)$ and $p^* \in \mu(z^*)$. Thus $0 \geqslant h(p^*) \cdot z^* \geqslant h(p) \cdot z^*$ for all $p \in K$, where the first inequality follows from Walras' law and the second from the definition of μ. In terms of D, the above becomes $h(p^*) \cdot z^* \geqslant q \cdot z^*$ for all $q \in D$ and so also for all $q \in C$. By 2.14(b), $z^* \in \gamma(p^*) \cap C^*$. The proof of compactness is routine.

21.8 Exercise: Corollary to 18.17 (Cornet [1975])
Let γ satisfy the hypotheses of 18.17 with $C = \mathbf{R}^m$ and relax the assumption of compact values to closed values. Then $\{p \in B : 0 \in \gamma(p)\}$ is compact and nonempty.

21.9 Exercise: Corollary 16.7 Implies Theorem 16.5 (Fan [1964])
Hint: Let f_i be the indicator function (2.31) of E_i.

21.10 Minimax Theorem 16.11 Implies the Equilibrium Theorem 8.3
Let $f : \Delta \to \mathbf{R}^m$ be continuous and satisfy $p \cdot f(p) \leqslant 0$. Let $g : \Delta \times \Delta \to \mathbf{R}$ be defined by $g(p,q) = p \cdot f(q)$. Then g is quasi-concave in p and continuous in q, and $\max_{p \in \Delta} g(p,p) \leqslant 0$ by Walras' law. By 16.11,

$$\min_q \max_p p \cdot f(q) \leqslant 0.$$

Thus there is some $\bar{q}$ such that for all $p \in \Delta$ $p \cdot f(\bar{q}) \leqslant 0$, which implies that $f(q) \leqslant 0$. (cf. 8.4.)

21.11 Minimax Theorem 16.11 Implies 7.5
Let U be a binary relation on K satisfying the hypotheses of 7.5. Let f be the indicator function of $Gr\ U$. Then f is quasi-concave in its second argument and lower semi-continuous in its first argument. Since $x \notin U(x)$, $f(x,x) = 0$. Interchanging the order of the arguments in the statement of 16.11 yields

$$\min_{z \in K} \sup_{y \in K} f(z,y) \leqslant \sup_{x \in K} f(x,x) = 0.$$

Thus there exists $\bar{z}$ such that $f(\bar{z},y) \leqslant 0$ for all y, i.e., $y \notin U(\bar{z})$ for all y. (In fact, all we need is that $U^{-1}(x)$ is open for any x, not that U has open graph.)

21.12 Exercise: Theorem 16.11 Implies 16.5 (Fan [1972])
Hint: Let f_i, X_i $i = 1,\ldots,n$ satisfy the hypotheses of 16.5. Set $X = \prod_{i=1}^{n} X_i$. Define $g : X \times X \to \mathbf{R}$ by

$$g(y,x) = \min_{i=1,\dots,n} f_i(x_{-i},y_i).$$

21.13 Remark
The maximum theorem and related results can be combined with the Kakutani fixed point theorem to provide generalizations of many of the previous results. A few examples follow. Some require other techniques.

21.14 Exercise: A Generalization of 8.1
For $i = 1,\dots,n$, let $K_i \subset \mathbf{R}^{k_i}$ be compact and convex. Let $f : \prod_{i=1}^n K_i \to \prod_{i=1}^n \mathbf{R}^{k_i}$ be continuous. Then there is some $\bar{p} = (\bar{p}^1, \dots, \bar{p}^n) \in \prod_{i=1}^n K_i$ satisfying

$$\bar{p}^i \cdot f^i(\bar{p}) \geqslant p^i \cdot f^i(\bar{p})$$

for all $p^i \in K_i$ and all $i = 1,\dots,n$, where $f^i(\bar{p})$ is the projection of $f(\bar{p})$ on $\mathbf{R}^{k_i}$.

21.15 Exercise: A Generalization of 17.6
For $i = 1,\dots,n$, let $K_i \subset \mathbf{R}^{k_i}$ be compact and convex and let $K = \prod_{i=1}^n K_i$. Let $\beta_i : K \twoheadrightarrow K_i$ be an upper hemi-continuous correspondence with closed convex values satisfying for each $x = (x^1,\dots,x^n) \in K$ there is a $\lambda_i > 0$ and $w^i \in \beta_i(x)$ such that

$$x^i + \lambda_i w^i \in K_i.$$

Then there is some $\bar{x} \in K$ such that $0 \in \beta_i(\bar{x})$ for all $i = 1,\dots,n$.

21.16 Exercise: A More General K-K-M Lemma
For each $i = 1,\dots,n$, let $K_i \subset \mathbf{R}^{k_i}$ be the convex hull of $\{x_1^i,\dots,x_{t_i}^i\}$. Set $K = \prod_{i=1}^n K_i$. For $i = 1,\dots,k$ and $j = 1,\dots,t_i$ let $F_j^i : K \twoheadrightarrow K^i$ be continuous correspondences with closed values satisfying for each $A \subset \{1,\dots,t_i\}$ and all $x \in K$,

$$co\ \{x_j^i : j \in A\} \subset \bigcup_{j \in A} F_j^i(x).$$

Then there exists some $\bar{x} \in K$ such that for each $i = 1,\dots,n$,

$$\bigcap_{j=1}^{t_i} F_j^i(\bar{x}) \neq \varnothing.$$

(Hint: The F_j^i's are not necessarily convex-valued so that none of our fixed point or approximation theorems apply. However, the set K is a product of closed simplexes, which has a very special structure. Generalize the argument of 9.2 using barycentric coordinates. The only difficulty is showing continuity of the g_j^i functions. Use 13.1.)

21.17 Exercise: The General Form of Peleg's Lemma (Peleg [1967]) For each $i = 1,\ldots,n$, let $K_i \subset \mathbf{R}^{k_i}$ be the convex hull of $\{x^i_1,\ldots,x^i_{t_i}\}$. Set $K = \prod_{i=1}^{n} K_i$. For each $x = (x^1,\ldots,x^n) \in K$ and each $i = 1,\ldots,n$ let $R_i(x)$ be an acyclic binary relation on $\{1,\ldots,t_i\}$ such that whenever the jth barycentric coordinate of $x^i = 0$, then j is $R^i(x)$-maximal. Assume further that for each $i = 1,\ldots,n$, and any $j,k \in \{1,\ldots,t_i\}$, that the set $\{x \in K : j \in R_i(x)(k)\}$ is open in K. Then there exists some $\bar{x} \in K$ satisfying $R_i(\bar{x}) = \varnothing$ for all $i = 1,\ldots,n$.

CHAPTER 22

The Knaster-Kuratowski-Mazurkiewicz-Shapley lemma

22.0 Note

The following generalizations of the K-K-M lemma (5.4) are due to Shapley [1973], who proved them for the case where the a^i's are all unit coordinate vectors. The method of proof given is due to Ichiishi [1981a].

22.1 Definition

Let $N = \{1,...,n\}$. A family β of nonempty subsets of N is *balanced* if for each $B \in \beta$, there is a nonnegative real number λ_B (called a *balancing weight*) such that for each $i \in N$,

$$\sum_{\beta(i)} \lambda_B = 1,$$

where $\beta(i) = \{B \in \beta : i \in B\}$.

22.2 Definition

Let $e^1, \dots, e^n$ be the unit coordinate vectors in $\mathbf{R}^n$. For each $B \subset N$, set $m_B = \frac{1}{|B|} \sum_{i \in B} e^i$.

22.3 Exercise

A family β is balanced if and only if $m_N \in co\ \{m_B : B \in \beta\}$.

22.4 K-K-M-S Lemma (Shapley [1973])

Let $\{a^i : i \in N\} \subset \mathbf{R}^m$ and let $\{F_B : B \subset N\}$ be a family of closed subsets of $\mathbf{R}^k$ such that for each nonempty $A \subset N$,

$$co\ \{a^i : i \in A\} \subset \bigcup_{B \subset A} F_B.$$

Then there is a balanced family β of subsets of N such that

$$\bigcap_{B \in \beta} F_B \text{ is nonempty and compact.}$$

22.5 Exercise

This theorem includes the K-K-M lemma by setting $F_B = \varnothing$ for B not a singleton.

22.6 Proof (Ichiishi [1981a])

Compactness is immediate. The nonemptiness proof will make use of the Fan-Browder theorem (17.1). Set $K = co\ \{a^i : i \in N\}$, and for $x \in K$ denote by $I(x)$ the collection $\{B \subset N : x \in F_B\}$. By hypothesis $I(x)$ is nonempty for all x. Let $\Delta = co\ \{e^i \in \mathbf{R}^n : i \in N\}$ and define $\sigma : \Delta \to K$ by $\sigma(z) = \sum_{i \in N} z_i a^i$. Define $\gamma : \Delta \twoheadrightarrow \Delta$ by

$$\gamma(z) = co\ \{m_B : B \in I(\sigma(z))\}.$$

Since each F_B is closed and σ is continuous, each z has a neighborhood V such that for all $w \in V$, $I(\sigma(w)) \subset I(\sigma(z))$. It follows that γ is upper hemi-continuous. Further, γ has nonempty compact convex values. Define $\mu : \Delta \twoheadrightarrow \Delta$ to be the constant correspondence

$$\mu(z) = \{m_N\}.$$

From Exercise 22.2, it suffices to show that there is a $\bar{z}$ such that $\gamma(\bar{z}) \cap \mu(\bar{z}) \neq \varnothing$, for then $\beta = I(\sigma(\bar{z}))$ is balanced and $\sigma(\bar{z}) \in \bigcap_{\beta} F_B$.

Let $z \in \Delta$, and let $A = \{i : z_i > 0\}$. Thus $\sigma(z) \in co\ \{a^i : i \in A\}$. Then by hypothesis, $\sigma(z) \in F_B$ for some $B \subset A$. Set $y^\lambda = z + \lambda(m_N - m_B)$. The hypotheses of 17.1 will be met if for some $\lambda > 0$, $y^\lambda \in \Delta$, i.e., if $\sum_{i \in N} y_i^\lambda = 1$ and $y^\lambda \geqslant 0$. Now,

$$y^\lambda = z + \lambda\left[\frac{1}{n}\sum_{i \in N} e^i - \frac{1}{|B|}\sum_{i \in B} e^i\right],$$

and so

$$y_i^\lambda = z_i + \frac{\lambda}{n} - \frac{\lambda}{|B|}\delta_B^i,$$

where

$$\delta_B^i = \begin{cases} 1 \text{ if } i \in B \\ 0 \text{ otherwise.} \end{cases}$$

But

$$\sum_{i \in N}\left[z_i + \frac{\lambda}{n} - \frac{\lambda}{|B|}\delta_B^i\right] = \sum_{i \in N} z_i = 1$$

and so $\sum_{i \in N} y_i^\lambda = 1$. For

$$0 < \lambda < \min_{i \in B} \frac{z_i}{\frac{1}{|B|} - \frac{1}{n}},$$

we have that

$$z_i + \frac{\lambda}{n} - \frac{\lambda}{|B|}\delta_B^i \geqslant 0$$

for all i. (Recall that for $i \in B$, $z_i > 0$ as $B \subset A$.) Thus by 17.1, there is a $\tilde{z}$ such that $\gamma(\tilde{z}) \cap \mu(\tilde{z}) \neq \emptyset$.

22.7 Definition

Let $N = \{1,...,n\}$ and let $\pi = \{\pi_B^i : i \in N; B \subset N\}$ be set of strictly positive numbers satisfying,

$$\text{for each } B \subset N, \ \sum_{i \in B} \pi_B^i = 1. \tag{22.8}$$

A family β of subsets of N is π-balanced if for each $B \in \beta$, there is a nonnegative real number λ_B (called a *π-balancing weight*) such that for each $i \in N$,

$$\sum_{\beta(i)} \pi_B^i \lambda_B = 1.$$

22.9 Exercise

For each $B \subset N$, set

$$m_B(\pi) = \frac{1}{|B|} \sum_{i \in B} \pi_B^i e^i.$$

Then a family β is π-balanced if and only if $m_N \in co\ \{m_B(\pi) : B \in \beta\}$. (Note that we use m_N not $m_N(\pi)$.)

22.10 Theorem (Shapley [1973])

Let $\{a^i: i \in N\} \subset \mathbf{R}^m$ and let $\{F_B: B \subset N\}$ be a family of closed subsets of $\mathbf{R}^m$ such that for each nonempty $A \subset N$,

$$co\ \{a^i : i \in A\} \subset \bigcup_{B \subset A} F_B.$$

Then for every set π of positive numbers satisfying 22.8, there is a π-balanced family β of subsets of N such that

$$\bigcap_{B \in \beta} F_B \text{ is nonempty and compact.}$$

22.11 Proof

The proof follows 22.6 and it is left as an exercise to make the necessary changes in that argument.

CHAPTER 23

Cooperative equilibria of games

23.0 Remarks and Definitions

This chapter examines notions of equilibria when players cooperate with each other in determining their strategies. The Nash equilibrium concept of Chapter 19 was based on the notion that players would only consider the effect of unilateral strategy changes in deciding whether or not they could be made better off. The cooperative theory takes into account that coalitions of players may have more power to make their members better off than they would be by acting individually. Three different approaches to the problem will be considered in this chapter. The first two approaches deal with games in what is known as their characteristic function form. The characteristic function approach to cooperative game theory takes as a primitive notion the set of payoffs that a coalition can guarantee for its members. These payoffs may be expressed either in physical terms or in utility terms. The utility characteristic function approach goes back to von Neumann and Morgenstern [1944].

For the remainder of this chapter, $N = \{1,...,n\}$ denotes the set of players. A *coalition* is a nonempty subset of N. Given a family of sets $\{X_i : i \in N\}$, let $X^B = \prod_{i \in B} X_i$. We will let X denote X^N when no confusion will result. We will also use the notation $\mathbf{R}^B = \prod_{i \in B} \mathbf{R}$. For $x \in X$ (resp. $x \in \mathbf{R}^N$), π^B will denote the projection of x on X^B (resp. $\mathbf{R}^B$).

A game in *utility characteristic function form* is a tuple $(N, (V^B), F)$ where $F \subset \mathbf{R}^N$ and for each coalition B, $V^B \subset \mathbf{R}^N$. The set F is the set of utility vectors that can result in the game. For $x \in F$, x_i is the numerical value of player i's utility. The set V^B is the set of utility vectors that coalition B can guarantee for its members. If $i \notin B$, then the fact that $x \in V^B$ does not impose any restriction on x_i. In general, $F = V^N$, but this is not necessary. The *core* of such a game is the set of all utility allocations that no coalition can improve upon. Coalition B can *improve upon* $x \in F$ if there is some $z \in V^B$ such that $z_i > x_i$ for each $i \in B$.

A shortcoming of this model is that the players have to have utility functions. If the players have preferences over outcomes which are not representable by utility functions, then the characteristic function must specify the physical outcomes that a coalition can guarantee for its members. The preferences can then be described as binary relations on vectors of physical outcomes and it is not necessary to rely on a utility function. A game in *outcome characteristic function form* is specified by a tuple $(N, (X_i), (F^B), F, (U_i))$, where for each coalition B, $F^B \subset X^B$; $F \subset X$; and for each $i \in N$, $U_i : X_i \twoheadrightarrow X_i$. Each X_i is a set of personal outcomes for player i. The set F^B is the set of vectors of outcomes for members of B that coalition B can guarantee. The set of vectors of outcomes that can actually occur is F, which again may or may not be equal to F^N. The preferences of player i are represented by the correspondence U_i, and they depend only on i's personal outcome. The definition of the core for this form of game is the set of physical outcomes that no coalition can improve upon. For an outcome characteristic function game, we say that coalition B can improve upon $x \in F$ if there is some $z^B \in F^B$ such that $z_i^B \in U_i(x_i)$ for each $i \in B$.

While the characteristic function form of a game can be taken as a primitive notion, it is also possible to derive characteristic functions from a game in strategic form. Let X_i be player i's strategy set and assume that each player's preferences are representable by a utility function $u^i : X \to \mathbf{R}$. Aumann and Peleg [1961] define an α-characteristic function and a β-characteristic function based on a strategic form game. The α-characteristic function is defined by

$$V_\alpha^B = \{w \in \mathbf{R}^N : \forall x \in X \ \exists z^B \in X^B \ \forall i \in B \ \ u^i(x|z^B) \geqslant w_i\}$$

The β-characteristic function is defined by

$$V_\beta^B = \{w \in \mathbf{R}^N : \exists z^B \in X^B \ \forall x \in X \ \forall i \in B \ \ u^i(x|z^B) \geqslant w_i\}$$

A third approach to cooperative equilibrium works directly with the strategic form and combines aspects of both the core and Nash equilibrium. Let us say that coalition B can improve upon strategy vector $x \in X$ if there is some $z^B \in X^B$ such that for all $i \in B$, $u^i(x|z^B) > u^i(x)$. A *strong Nash equilibrium* of a game in strategic form is a strategy vector x that no coalition can improve upon.

Theorem 23.5 below is due to Scarf [1967] for the case of $F = F^N$

and gives sufficient conditions for a utility-characteristic function game to have a nonempty core. The statement and proof given are due to Shapley [1973]. Theorem 23.6 is due to Border [1982] and proves a similar result for outcome-characteristic function games. The technique of the proof was suggested by Ichiishi [1981b]. Scarf [1971] shows that for a strategic form game where players have continuous utilities that are quasi-concave in the strategy vectors, then the α-characteristic function game it generates satisfies the hypotheses of 23.5 and so has a nonempty core. The same cannot be said for the β-characteristic function. Theorem 23.7 is a variant of a theorem of Ichiishi [1982] and provides conditions under which a strategic form game possesses a strong equilibrium. All three of these theorems are based on a *balancedness* hypothesis. There are two notions of balancedness for games in characteristic function form, corresponding to utility characteristic function games and outcome characteristic games, which we shall call U-balance and O-balance, and which are crucial to proving nonemptiness of the core. They require the feasibility of a particular vector if it is related in the appropriate way to a family of vectors which are coalitionally feasible for a balanced family (22.1) of coalitions. The notion of S-balance refers to games in strategic form and is a very strong restriction on the preferences of the players.

A good example of a game in outcome characteristic function form is given by Boehm's [1974] model of a coalitional production economy. Each consumer $i \in N$ has a consumption set X_i and endowment w_i. Each coalition B has a production set Y^B. The total production set is Y. An *allocation* is an $x \in X$ satisfying $\sum_{i \in N} x_i - \sum_{i \in N} w_i \in Y$. Boehm allows for Y to be different from Y^N, which he argues might result from decreasing returns to cooperation. An outcome for consumer i is just a consumption vector x_i. Let i's preferences over consumption vectors be represented by a correspondence $U_i : X_i \twoheadrightarrow X_i$. Coalition B can block allocation x if there is some $z^B \in X^B$ satisfying $\sum_{i \in B} z_i^B - \sum_{i \in B} w_i \in Y^B$ and $z_i^B \in U_i(x_i)$ for all $i \in B$. That is, coalition B can take its aggregate endowment and produce a consumption vector for its members which they all prefer. The core of the economy is the set of all unblocked allocations. Boehm proves the nonemptiness of the core of a coalitional production economy when consumers have continuous quasi-concave utility functions and the technology is balanced in a certain sense. Theorem 23.13 below shows that the assumption of ordered preferences can be dropped if we are willing to make the additional assumption that the total production set Y is convex.

23.1 Definition
A utility characteristic function game is *U-balanced* if for every balanced family β of coalitions, if $\pi^B(x) \in V^B$ for each $B \in \beta$, then $x \in V(N)$. Another way to state this is that

$$\bigcap_{B \varepsilon \beta} V(B) \subset V(N).$$

23.2 Definition
An outcome characteristic function game is *O-balanced* if for any balanced family β of coalitions with balancing weights $\{\lambda_B\}$ satisfying $x^B \in F^B$ for each $B \in \beta$, then $x \in F$, where $x_i = \sum_{B \varepsilon \beta(i)} \lambda_B x_i^B$.

23.3 Definition
A strategic form game is *S-balanced* if for any balanced family β of coalitions with balancing weights $\{\lambda_B\}$ satisfying $u^i(x^B) > w_i$ for all $i \in B$, then $u^i(x) \geqslant w_i$ for all $i \in N$, where $x_i = \sum_{B \varepsilon \beta(i)} \lambda_B x_i^B$.

23.4 Remark
Since $x_i = \sum_{B \varepsilon \beta(i)} \lambda_B \pi_i^B(x)$, O-balancedness is a stronger requirement than U-balancedness.

23.5 Theorem (cf. Scarf [1967])
Let $G = (N, (V^B), F)$ be a utility-characteristic function game satisfying

23.5.1. $V(\{i\}) = \{x \in \mathbf{R}^n : x_i \leqslant 0\}$.

For each coalition $B \subset N$,

23.5.2. $V(B)$ is closed and nonempty and comprehensive, i.e., $y \leqslant x \in V(B) \Rightarrow y \in V(B)$. Also if $x \in V(B)$ and $x_i = y_i$ for all $i \in B$, then $y \in V(B)$.

23.5.3. F is closed and $x \in V(N)$ implies there exists $y \in F$ with $x \leqslant y$.

23.5.4. There is a real number M such that for each coalition $B \subset N$,

$$i \in B \text{ and } x \in V(B) \text{ imply } x_i \leqslant M.$$

23.5.5. G is U-balanced.

Then the core of G is nonempty.

23.6 Theorem (Border [1982])
Let $G = (N, (X_i), (F^B), (U_i))$ be an outcome characteristic game satisfying:

23.6.1. For each i, X_i is a nonempty convex subset of $\mathbf{R}^{k_i}$.
23.6.2. $B \subset N$, F^B is a nonempty compact subset of X^B.
23.6.3. F is convex and compact.
23.6.4. For each i,
 (a) U_i has open graph in $X_i \times X_i$,
 (b) $x_i \notin U_i(x_i)$.
 (c) $U_i(x_i)$ is convex (but possibly empty).
23.6.5. G is O-balanced.
Then the core of G is nonempty.

23.7 Theorem (cf. Ichiishi [1982])
Let $G = (N, (X_i), (u_i))$ be a strategic form game satisfying
23.7.1. For each i, X_i is a nonempty compact convex subset of $\mathbf{R}^{k_i}$.
23.7.2. For each i, $u^i : X \to \mathbf{R}$ is continuous.
23.7.3. G is S-balanced.
Then G has a strong equilibrium.

23.8 Proof of Theorem 23.5 (Shapley [1973])
Let (N,F,V) be a balanced game and let M be as in 23.5.4. Put $g^i = -nMe^i$, where e^i is the ith unit coordinate vector in $\mathbf{R}^N$. Put $K = co\,\{g^i : i \in N\}$. Define $\tau : \mathbf{R}^N \to \mathbf{R}$ by

$$\tau(x) = \max\,\{t : x + tu \in \bigcup_{B \subset N} V(B)\},$$

where u is a vector of ones. For each x, $\tau(x)$ is finite by 23.5.4 and τ is continuous by 23.5.2 and an argument similar to the proof of the maximum theorem (12.1). For each coalition B define

$$F_B = \{x \in K : x + \tau(x)u \in V(B)\}.$$

Suppose the points $\{g^i\}$ and sets $\{F_B\}$ satisfy the hypotheses of the K-K-M-S lemma (22.4). Then there is a balanced family β such that $\bigcap_{B \in \beta} F_B \neq \varnothing$. Let $\tilde{x}$ belong to this intersection and put $\tilde{y} = \tilde{x} + \tau(\tilde{x})u$. Then $\tilde{y} \in \bigcap_{B \in \beta} V(B)$ but belongs to $int\, V(A)$ for no A. Since the game is balanced, $\tilde{y} \in V(N)$. Thus by 23.5.3 there is a $\tilde{z} \in F$ with $\tilde{y} \leqslant \tilde{z}$. Such a $\tilde{z}$ belongs to the core.

To verify the hypotheses of the K-K-M-S lemma (22.4), we first observe that each F_B is closed. Next we show that $co\,\{g^i : i \in A\} \subset \bigcup_{B \subset A} F_B$ for each $A \subset N$. Note that since each $x \in K$ belongs to some F_B, it suffices to prove that

$$x \in F_B \cap co\,\{g^i : i \in A\} \text{ implies } B \subset A.$$

Since $B \subset N$ for all B, assume that $A \neq N$. Then $|A| < n$. But $x \in co\,\{g^i : i \in A\}$ implies $\sum_{i \in A} x_i = -nM$; but for some $k \in A$, x_k

must be less than or equal to the average, i.e.,

$$x_k \leqslant -\frac{n}{|A|}M < -M.$$

Thus by the definition of F_B, $x \in F_B$ implies $x + \tau(x)u \in F_B$, and since $x_k < -M$, we must have $\tau(x) > M$. Otherwise the maximum in the definition of τ would occur for $V(\{k\})$, which would be larger than $\tau(x)$. Similarly, $x + \tau(x)u$ is not in the interior of any $V(C)$, $C \subset N$; in particular, $x + \tau(x)u \notin int\ V(\{i\})$ for any $i \in B$, so $x + \tau(x)u \in F_B$. By 23.5.4, $x_i + \tau(x) \leqslant M$ for all $i \in B$; but $\tau(x) \geqslant M$, so $x_i < 0$ for all $i \in B$. But if $x \in co\ \{g^i : i \in A\}$, then $x_i = 0$ if $i \notin A$. Thus $B \subset A$.

23.9 Proof of Theorem 23.6

As in 22.3, define $v_i = X_i \times X_i \to \mathbf{R}_+$ by

$$v_i(y_i,x_i) = dist\ [(x_i,y_i),(Gr\ U_i)^c].$$

Each v_i is continuous (as $Gr\ U_i$ is open) and $v_i(y_i,x_i) > 0$ if and only if $y_i \in U_i(x_i)$. The function v_i is also quasi-concave in its first argument. That is if $v_i(z_i^k,x_i) \geqslant w$ for $k = 1,\ldots,p$ and if z_i be a convex combination of $z_i^1,\ldots,z_i^k$, then $v_i(z_i,x_i) \geqslant w$. The proof of this is in section 23.10.

For each coalition B, set

$$V^B(x) = \{w \in \mathbf{R}^N : \exists z^B \varepsilon F^B \quad \forall i \varepsilon B \quad w_i \leqslant v_i(z_i^B, x_i)\}.$$

If $i \notin B$, then $w \in V^B(x)$ places no restriction on w_i. Thus x is in the core if and only if $x \in F$ and $\bigcup_{B \subset N} V^B(x) \cap \mathbf{R}^N_{++} = \varnothing$.

The sets $V^B(x)$ are analogues of the utility characteristic function and the previous sorts of arguments may be applied. The following line of argument is similar to Ichiishi [1981b].

Since each v_i is continuous and each F^B is compact, there is some $M \geqslant 0$ such that for all $x \in X$, and $z^B \in F^B$, $v_i(z_i^B, x_i) \leqslant M$ for all $i \in B$. Put $a^i = -nMe^i \in \mathbf{R}^N$ (where e^i is the ith unit coordinate vector of $\mathbf{R}^N$) and set $K = co\ \{a^i = i \in N\}$. For each $B \subset N$ set $m_B = \frac{1}{|B|}\sum_{i \varepsilon B} a^i$.

For each $y \in K$ set $\tau(y,x) = \max\ \{t > 0 : y + tu \in \bigcup_{B \subset N} V^B(x)\}$, where u is a vector of ones, and put $w(y,x) = y + \tau(y,x)u$. Note that $\tau(y,x) < M(n + 1)$ and $w(y,x) \leqslant Mu$. Since v_i is always nonnegative, $V^{\{k\}}(x)$ always includes $\{w : w_k \leqslant 0\}$. Suppose that some $w_k(y,x) < 0$, then $w(y,x) = y + \tau(y,x)u$ is in the interior of $V^{\{k\}}(x)$, which contradicts the definition of τ. Thus $w(y,x) \geqslant 0$.

The next step is to show that if $x \in F$ and $w(y,x) \leqslant 0$, then x is in the core. Suppose not. Then for some $z^B \in F^B$, $z_i^B \in U_i(x)$ for all $i \in B$, so $v_i(z_i^B,x_i) > 0$ for all $i \in B$. Thus there is a $w \in V^B(x)$ with $w > 0$. But then $y + \tau(y,x)u = w(y,x) \leqslant 0$ is in the interior of $V^B(x)$, which contradicts the definition of τ.

Thus the search for a member of the core has been reduced to the following problem: Find $x \in F$ and $y \in K$ such that $w(y,x) \leqslant 0$. To this end make the following constructions. For each $B \in N$, set $\Gamma^B(x) = \{y \in K : w(y,x) \in V^B(x)\}$. Define $E(x,y) = \{z \in F : z \text{ minimizes } dist\ [v(\cdot,x), \{w : w \geqslant w(y,x)\}]\}$, where the ith component of $v(x,y)$ is $v_i(x_i,y_i)$.

Define $\gamma,\mu : F \times K \twoheadrightarrow F \times K$ by

$$\gamma(x,y) = \{x\} \times co\ \{m_B : y \in \Gamma^B(x)\}$$

and

$$\mu(x,y) = co\ E(x,y) \times \{m_N\}.$$

The correspondences γ and μ so defined satisfy the hypotheses of Theorem 17.1. The proof of this claim is given in Section 23.11. It follows then that there are $\bar{x}$, $\bar{y}$, x^*, y^* satisfying

$$(\bar{x},\bar{y}) \in \mu(x^*,y^*) \cap \gamma(x^*,y^*).$$

In other words,

$$\bar{x} \in co\ E(x^*,y^*). \tag{1}$$

$$\bar{y} = m_N. \tag{2}$$

$$\bar{x} = x^*. \tag{3}$$

$$\bar{y} \in co\ \{m_B : y^* \in \Gamma^B(x^*)\}. \tag{4}$$

By (2) and (4) and 22.3, $\beta = \{B : y^* \in \Gamma^B(x^*)\}$ is balanced, and by the definition of Γ, $w(y^*,x^*) \in V^B(x^*)$ for all $B \in \beta$. Thus for each $B \in \beta$ there exists $z^B \in F^B$ satisfying $w_i(y^*,x^*) \leqslant v_i(z_i^B,x_i^*)$ for all $i \in B$. Let $\{\lambda_B\}$ be the balancing weights associated with β. Since the game is balanced, $z^* \in F$ where

$$z_i^* = \sum_{B \in \beta(i)} \lambda_B z_i^B.$$

Since z_i^* is a convex combination of the z_i^B vectors, for $i \in B$, and $v_i(z_i^B,x_i^*) \geqslant w_i(y^*,x^*)$, it follows from quasi-concavity that $v_i(z_i^*,x_i^*) \geqslant w_i(y^*,x^*)$.

By (1) and (3), $x^* \in co\ E(x^*,y^*)$. Since $z^* \in F$ and $v(z^*,x^*) \geqslant w(y^*,x^*)$, if $z \in E(x^*,y^*)$, then $v(z,x^*) \geqslant w(y^*,x^*)$. Suppose that $w_i(y^*,x^*) > 0$. Then for all $z \in E(x^*,y^*)$, $v_i(z_i,x_i^*) > 0$ as well. Thus $z_i \in U_i(x_i^*)$. Thus $x^* \in co\ E(x^*,y^*)$ implies that $x_i^* \in U_i(x_i^*)$, a contradiction. Thus $w(y^*,x^*) \leqslant 0$. Also since F is convex and $E(x^*,y^*) \subset F$, it follows that $x^* \in F$. Thus x^* is in the core.

23.10 Quasi-concavity of v_i in Its First Argument

Let $v_i(z_i^k,x_i) \geqslant w$, $k = 1,\ldots,p$ and let $z_i = \sum_{k=1}^{p} \lambda_k z_i^k$ be a convex combination $z_i^1,\ldots,z_i^p$. Then $v_i(z_i,x_i) \geqslant w$.

For convenience, the common subscript i will be omitted. If $w \leqslant 0$, the result is trivial. If $w > 0$, let $N_w(x,z^k)$ be the open ball of radius w about (x,z^k). From the definition of v, $N_w(x,z^k) \subset Gr\ U$, $k = 1,\ldots,p$. Let $(x',z') \in N_w(x,z)$. Then $|(x' - x, z' - z)| < w$ so $(x + (x' - x), z^k + (z' - z)) \in N_w(x,z^k) \subset Gr\ U$. Thus $z^k + z' - z \in U(x')$. Since $U(x')$ is convex, $z' = \sum_{k=1}^{p} \lambda_k(z^k + z' - z) \in U(x')$. Thus $N_w(x,z) \subset Gr\ U$, so $v(z,x) \geqslant w$.

23.11 The Correspondences γ and μ Satisfy the Hypotheses of Theorem 17.1

It is straightforward to verify that γ and μ are upper hemi-continuous with nonempty compact convex values. It is harder to see that for every $(x,y) \in X \times K$, there exist $(x',y') \in \mu(x,y)$, $(x'',y'') \in \gamma(x,y)$ and $\bar{\lambda} > 0$ satisfying $(x,y) + \bar{\lambda}[(x',y') - (x'',y'')] \in X \times K$. The argument is virtually identical to one used by Ichiishi [1981] with only slightly different correspondences. Put $x'' = x$, $y' = m_N$ and choose any $x' \in co\ E(x,y)$. Then $x + \lambda(x' - x'') = (1 - \lambda)x + \lambda x' \in X$ for any $\lambda \in [0,1]$. Let $B \subset N = \{i : y_i > 0\}$. It follows just as in 23.8 that $co\ \{a^i : i \in B\} \subset \bigcup_{C \subset B} \Gamma^C(x)$. Given this, choose $C \subset B$ so that $y \in \Gamma^C(x)$. Put $y'' = m_C$. Then $(x'',y'') \in \gamma(x,y)$. For $\lambda \in [0,1]$, define $y^\lambda = y + \lambda(y' - y'') = y + \lambda(m_N - m_C)$. Then

$$\begin{aligned}\sum_{i \in N} y_i^\lambda &= \sum_{i \in N} y_i + \lambda\Big(\sum_{i \in N}(m_N)_i - \sum_{i \in N}(m_C)_i\Big)\\ &= -nM + \lambda(-nM + nM)\\ &= -nM.\end{aligned}$$

If $(y' - y'')_i = (m_N - m_C)_i > 0$, then $i \in C \subset B$, so $y_i < 0$. Thus for $\bar{\lambda}$ small enough, $y^{\bar{\lambda}} \leqslant 0$, so $y^{\bar{\lambda}} \in K$.

23.12 Proof of Theorem 23.7 (cf. Ichiishi [1981b, 1982], Border [1982])

The proof is nearly identical to the proof of Theorem 23.6 given in 23.9, so it will be sketched here. The details are left as an exercise.

For each coalition B, set

$$V^B(x) = \{w \in \mathbf{R}^N : \exists z^B \in X^B \quad \forall i \in B \quad u^i(x|z^B) \geqslant w_i\}.$$

Define K, τ, $w(y,x)$ as in 23.9 and set

$$E(x,y) = co\ \{z \in X : z \text{ minimizes } dist\ [u(\cdot), \{w : w \geqslant w(y,x)\}]\},$$

where the ith component of $u(z)$ is $u^i(z)$. Use 17.1 to find x^*, y^*, and a balanced family β of coalitions with balancing weights $\{\lambda_B\}$, such that for each $B \in \beta$, there is a $z^B \in X^B$ satisfying

$$u^i(x^*|z^B) \geqslant w_i(y^*,x^*)$$

for all $i \in B$. Since G is S-balanced, z^* defined by $z_i^* = \sum_{B \varepsilon \beta(i)} \lambda_B z_i^B$ satisfies $u^i(z^*) \geqslant w_i(y^*,x^*)$ for all $i \in N$. Conclude that $u^i(x^*) \geqslant w_i(y^*,x^*)$ for all $i \in N$ and hence that x^* is a strong equilibrium.

23.13 Theorem (Border [1982]; cf. Boehm [1974])

Let $(N, (X_i,w_i,U_i), (y^B), Y)$ be a coalitional production economy satisfying

23.13.1. For each i, $X_i \subset \mathbf{R}^m$ is closed, convex and bounded from below and $w_i \in X_i$.

23.13.2. For each i,

(a) U_i has open graph in $X_i \times X_i$.

(b) $x_i \notin U_i(x_i)$.

(c) $U_i(x_i)$ is convex.

23.13.3. For each coalition B, Y^B is closed and $0 \in Y^B$.

23.13.4. Y is closed and convex and $\mathbf{A}Y \cap \mathbf{R}_+^m = \{0\}$.

23.13.5. For every balanced family β of coalitions with balancing weights $\{\lambda_B\}$,

$$\sum_{B \varepsilon \beta} \lambda_B Y^B \subset Y.$$

Then the core of the economy is nonempty.

23.14 Proof

Exercise. Hint: Set

$$F^B = \left\{x^B \in X^B : \sum_{i \varepsilon B} x_i^B - \sum_{i \varepsilon B} w_i \in Y^B\right\}$$

and set

$$F = \left\{ x \in X : \sum_{i \in N} x_i - \sum_{i \in N} w_i \in Y \right\}.$$

Use balancedness to show that $\mathbf{A}Y^B \subset \mathbf{A}Y$. (Recall that $\mathbf{A}Y$ is the asymptotic cone of Y.) Use an argument similar to 20.3 to show that F and each F^B are compact. The convexity of Y implies the convexity of F, and 23.13.5 implies 0-balancedness. The result is then a direct consequence of 23.6.

References

Aliprantis, C. D. and Brown, D. J. 1983. "Equilibria in Markets with a Riesz Space of Commodities" *Journal of Mathematical Economics, 11*, 189-207.

Anderson, R. M. 1977. "Star-Finite Probability Theory" Ph.D. dissertation, Yale University.

Arrow, K. J. 1969. "Tullock and an Existence Theorem" *Public Choice, 6*, 105-111.

Arrow, K. J. and Debreu, G. 1954. "Existence of an Equilibrium for a Competitive Economy" *Econometrica, 22*, 265-290.

Arrow, K. J. and Hahn, F. 1971. *General Competitive Analysis.* San Francisco: Holden-Day.

Aumann, R. J. and Peleg, B. 1960. "Von Neumann-Morgenstern Solutions to Cooperative Games without Side Payments" *Bulletin of the American Mathematical Society, 66*, 173-179.

Berge, C. 1959. *Espaces topologiques et fonctions multivoques.* Paris: Dunod. [Translation: *Topological Spaces.* New York: Macmillan, 1963.]

Bergstrom, T. C. 1975. "Maximal Elements of Acyclic Relations on Compact Sets" *Journal of Economic Theory, 10*, 403-404.

1976. "How to Discard 'Free Disposability' - At No Cost" *Journal of Mathematical Economics, 3*, 131-134.

Bergstrom, T. C., Parks, R. P., and Rader, T. 1976. "Preferences Which Have Open Graphs" *Journal of Mathematical Economics, 3*, 313-316.

Bewley, T. 1972. "Existence of Equilibria in Economies with Infinitely Many Commodities" *Journal of Economic Theory, 4*, 414-540.

Boehm, V. 1974. "The Core of an Economy with Production" *Review of Economic Studies, 41*, 429-436.

Border, K. C. 1982. "The Core of a Coalitional Production Economy" Social Science Working Paper No 461, California Institute of Technology.

Borel, E. 1921. "La theorie du jeu et les equations integrales a noyeau symmetrique" *Comptes Rendus de l'Academie des Sciences, 173*, 1304-1308. [Translation: Savage, L. J. 1953. "The Theory of Play and Integral Equations with Skew Symmetric Kernels" *Econometrica, 21*, 97-100.]

Borglin, A. and Keiding, H. 1976. "Existence of Equilibrium Actions and of Equilibrium: A Note on the 'New' Existence Theorems" *Journal of Mathematical Economics, 3*, 313-316.

Borsuk, K. 1967. *Theory of Retracts.* Warsaw: Polish Scientific Publishers.

Bouligand, G. 1932. "Sur la semi-continuitè d'inclusion et quelques sujets connexes" *L'enseignement Mathèmatique, 31*, 14-22.

Brouwer, L. E. J. 1912. "Uber Abbildung von Mannigfaltikeiten" *Mathematische Annalen, 71*, 97-115.

Browder, F. E. 1967. "A New Generalization of the Schauder Fixed Point Theorem"

Mathematische Annalen, 174, 285-290.
1968. "The Fixed Point Theory of Multi-valued Mappings in Topological Vector Spaces" *Mathematische Annalen, 177*, 283-301.
1977. "On a Sharpened Form of the Schauder Fixed Point Theorem" *Proceedings of the National Academy of Sciences, USA, 74*, 4749-4751.
Brown, D. J. 1973. "Acyclic Choice" Cowles Foundation Discussion Paper No. 360, Yale University, mimeo.
1982. Personal Communication.
Cellina, A. 1969. "Approximation of Set-Valued Functions and Fixed Point Theorems" *Annali di Matematica Pura ed Applicata, 4*, 17-24.
Cohen, D. I. A. 1967. "On the Sperner Lemma" *Journal of Combinatorial Theory, 2*, 585-587.
Cornet, B. 1975. "Fixed Point and Surjectivity Theorems for Correspondences: Applications" Working Paper No. 7521, University of Paris-Dauphine.
Cottle, R. W. 1966. "Nonlinear Programs with Positively Bounded Jacobians" *SIAM Journal of Applied Mathematics, 14*, 147-158.
Debreu, G. 1952. "A Social Equilibrium Existence Theorem" *Proceedings of the National Academy of Sciences, 38*, 386-393.
1956. "Market Equilibrium" *Proceedings of the National Academy of Sciences, 42*, 876-878.
1959. *Theory of Value.* New York: Wiley.
1962. "New Concepts and Techniques for Equilibrium Analysis" *International Economic Review, 3*, 257-273.
1982. "Existence of Competitive Equilibrium" Chapter 15 in *Handbook of Mathematical Economics, vol. II*, edited by M. D. Intrilligator and K. J. Arrow. Amsterdam: North-Holland.
Dugundji, J. and Granas, A. 1978. "KKM-Maps and Variational Inequalities" *Annali della Scuola Normale Superiore di Pisa, Serie IV, 5*, 679-682.
1982. *Fixed Point Theory, vol. I.* Warsaw: Polish Scientific Publishers.
Eilenberg, S. and Montgomery, D. 1946. "Fixed Point Theorems for Multivalued Transformations" *American Journal of Mathematics, 68*, 214-222.
Fan, K. 1952. "Fixed-Point and Minimax Theorems in Locally Convex Topological Linear Spaces" *Proceedings of the National Academy of Sciences, USA, 38*, 121-126.
1961. "A Generalization of Tychonoff's Fixed Point Theorem" *Mathematische Annalen, 142*, 305-310.
1964. "Sur un thèorème minimax" *Comptes Rendus de l'Academie des Sciences de Paris, Groupe 1, 259*, 3925-3928.
1969. "Extensions of Two Fixed Point Theorems of F.E. Browder" *Mathematische Zeitschrift, 112*, 234-240.
1972. "A Minimax Inequality and Applications" In *Inequalities - III*, edited by O. Shisha. New York: Academic Press.
Gaddum, J. W. 1952. "A Theorem on Convex Cones with Applications to Linear Inequalities" *Proceedings of the American Mathematical Society, 3*, 957-960.
Gale, D. 1955. "The Law of Supply and Demand" *Mathematica Scandinavica, 3*, 155-169.
1960. *The Theory of Linear Economic Models.* New York: McGraw-Hill.
Gale, D. and Mas-Colell, A. 1975. "An Equilibrium Existence Theorem for a General Model without Ordered Preferences" *Journal of Mathematical Economics, 2*, 9-15.
1979. "Corrections to an Equilibrium Existence Theorem for a General Model without Ordered Preferences" *Journal of Mathematical Economics, 6*, 297-

298.

Geistdoerfer-Florenzano, M. 1982. "The Gale-Nikaido-Debreu Lemma and the Existence of Transitive Equilibrium with or without the Free Disposal Assumption" *Journal of Mathematical Economics, 9*, 113-134.

Granas, A. 1981. "KKM-Maps and their Applications to Nonlinear Problems" In *The Scottish Book: Mathematics from the Scottish Cafe*, edited by R. D. Mauldin. Boston: Birkhauser.

Grandmont, J. M. 1977. "Temporary General Equilibrium Theory" *Econometrica, 45*, 535-572.

Green, E. 1981. Personal communication.

1984. "Continuum and Finite-Player Noncooperative Models of Competition" *Econometrica, 52*, 975-993.

Halpern, B. R. 1968. "A General Fixed Point Theorem" In *Proceedings of the Symposium on Nonlinear Functional Analysis*, American Mathematical Society, Providence.

Halpern, B. R. and Bergman, G. M. 1968. "A Fixed Point Theorem for Inward and Outward Maps" *Transactions of the American Mathematical Society, 130*, 353-358.

Hart, O. and Kuhn, H. W. 1975. "A Proof of the Existence of Equilibrium without the Free Disposal Assumption" *Journal of Mathematical Economics, 2*, 335-343.

Hartman, P. and Stampacchia, G. 1966. "On Some Non-linear Elliptic Differential-Functional Equations" *Acta Mathematica, 115*, 271-310.

Hildenbrand, W. 1974. *Core and Equilibria of a Large Economy*, Princeton University Press, Princeton.

Hildenbrand, W. and Kirman, A. 1976. *Introduction to Equilibrium Analysis*. Amsterdam: North-Holland.

Ichiishi, T. 1981a. "On the Knaster-Kuratowski-Mazurkiewicz-Shapley Theorem" *Journal of Mathematical Analysis and Applications, 81*, 297-299.

1981b. "A Social Coalitional Equilibrium Existence Theorem" *Econometrica, 49*, 369-377.

1982. "Non-cooperation and Cooperation" In *Games, Economic Dynamics, and Time Series Analysis*, edited by M. Deistler, E. Fürst, and G. Schwödiauer, Physica-Verlag, Vienna.

1983. *Game Theory for Economic Analysis*. New York: Academic Press.

Kakutani, S. 1941. "A Generalization of Brouwer's Fixed Point Theorem" *Duke Mathematical Journal, 8*, 416-427.

Karamardian, S. 1971. "Generalized Complementarity Problem" *Journal of Optimization Theory and Applications, 8*, 161-167.

Knaster, B., Kuratowski, K., and Mazurkiewicz, S. 1929. "Ein Beweis des Fixpunktsatze fur n-dimensionale Simplexe" *Fundamenta Mathematica, 14*, 132-137.

Koopmans, T. C. 1957. *Three Essays on the State of Economic Science*. New York: McGraw-Hill.

Kuhn, H. W. 1956. "A Note on 'The Law of Supply and Demand'" *Mathematica Scandinavica, 4*, 143-146.

1968. "Simplicial Approximation of Fixed Points" *Proceedings of the National Academy of Sciences, 61*, 1238-1242.

Kuratowski, K. 1932. "Les fonctions semi-continues dans l'espace des ensembles fermès" *Fundamenta Mathematica, 18*, 148-159.

1972. *Introduction to Set Theory and Topology*, 2nd ed. Oxford: Pergamon Press.

Le Van, C. 1982. "Topological Degree and the Sperner Lemma" *Journal of Optimization Theory and Applications, 37*, 371-377.

Luce, R. D. and Raiffa, H. 1957. *Games and Decisions.* New York: Wiley.
Mas-Colell, A. 1974. "An Equilibrium Existence Theorem without Complete or Transitive Preferences" *Journal of Mathematical Economics, 1*, 237-246.
1975. "A Model of Equilibrium with Differentiated Commodities" *Journal of Mathematical Economics, 2*, 263-295.
McCabe, P. J. 1981. "On Two Market Equilibrium Theorems" *Journal of Mathematical Economics, 8*, 167-171.
McKenzie, L. W. 1955. "Competitive Equilibrium with Dependent Preferences" In *Proceedings of the Second Symposium in Linear Programming*, edited by H. A. Antosiewicz, National Bureau of Standards, Washington.
1959. "On the Existence of General Equilibrium for a Competitive Market" *Econometrica, 27*, 54-71.
1961. "On the Existence of General Equilibrium: Some Corrections" *Econometrica, 29*, 247-248.
1981. "The Classical Theorem on Existence of Competitive Equilibrium" *Econometrica, 49*, 819-841.
Michael, E. 1956. "Continuous Selections I" *Annals of Mathematics, 63*, 361-382.
Moore, J. 1968. "A Note on Point-Set Mappings" In *Papers in Quantitative Economics 1*, edited by J. Quirk and A. Zarley, University of Kansas Press, Lawrence, Kansas.
1975. "The Existence of 'Compensated Equilibrium' and the Structure of the Pareto Efficiency Frontier" *International Economic Review, 16*, 167-300.
Moulin, H. 1982. *Game Theory for the Social Sciences.* New York: New York University Press.
Nash, J. 1950. "Equilibrium Points in N-person Games" *Proceedings of the National Academy of Sciences, 36*, 48-49.
Negishi, T. 1960. "Welfare Economics and Existence of an Equilibrium for a Competitive Economy" *Metroeconomica, 12*, 92-97.
Neuefeind, W. 1980. "Notes on Existence of Equilibrium Proofs and the Boundary Behavior of Supply" *Econometrica, 48*, 1831-1837.
Nikaido, H. 1956. "On the Classical Multilateral Exchange Problem" *Metroeconomica, 8*, 135-145.
1968. *Convex Structures and Economic Theory.* New York: Academic Press.
Owen, G. 1982. *Game Theory*, 2nd ed. New York: Academic Press.
Peleg, B. 1967. "Equilibrium Points for Open Acyclic Relations" *Canadian Journal of Mathematics, 19*, 366-369.
Prabhakar, N. D. and Yannelis, N. C. 1983. "Equilibrium in Abstract Economies with an Infinite Number of Agents, an Infinite Number of Commodities and without Ordered Preferences" Wayne State University, mimeo.
Rockafellar, R. T. 1970. *Convex Analysis.* Princeton: Princeton University Press.
Rudin, W. 1976. *Principles of Mathematical Analysis*, 3rd ed. New York: McGraw-Hill.
Scarf, H. E. 1967. "The Core of an N Person Game" *Econometrica, 35*, 50-69.
1971. "On the Existence of a Cooperative Solution for a General Class of *N*-Person Games" *Journal of Economic Theory, 3*, 169-181.
1973. *The Computation of Economic Equilibria.* New Haven: Yale University Press.
Shafer, W. J. 1974. "The Nontransitive Consumer" *Econometrica, 42*, 913-919.
1976. "Equilibrium in Economies without Ordered Preferences or Free Disposal" *Journal of Mathematical Economics, 3*, 135-137.
Shafer, W. J. and Sonnenschein, H. 1975. "Equilibrium in Abstract Economics without Ordered Preferences" *Journal of Mathematical Economics, 2*, 345-

348.
1976. "Equilibrium in Economies with Externalities, Commodity Taxation, and Lump Sum Transfers" *International Economic Review, 17*, 601-611.

Shapley, L. S. 1973. "On Balanced Games without Side Payments" In *Mathematical Programming*, edited by T. C. Hu and S. M. Robinson. New York: Academic Press.

Sion, M. 1958. "On General Minimax Theorems" *Pacific Journal of Mathematics, 8*, 171-176.

Sloss, J. L. 1971. "Stable Points of Directional Preference Relations" Technical Report No. 71-7, Operations Research House, Stanford University.

Sonnenschein, H. 1971. "Demand Theory without Transitive Preferences, with Applications to the Theory of Competitive Equilibrium" Chapter 10 in *Preferences, Utility, and Demand*, ed. by J. S. Chipman, L. Hurwicz, M. K. Richter, and H. F. Sonnenschein. New York: Harcourt Brace Jovanovich.

1977. "Some Recent Results on the Existence of Equilibrium in Finite Purely Competitive Economies" In *Frontiers of Quantitative Economics, Volume IIIA*, edited by M. D. Intrilligator. Amsterdam: North-Holland.

Sperner, E. 1928. "Neuer Beweis fur die Invarianz der Dimensionszahl und des Gebietes" *Abhandlungen aus dem Mathematischen Seminar der Hamburgischen Universitat, 6*, 265-272.

Todd, M. J. 1976. *The Computation of Fixed Points and Applications.* Berlin: Springer-Verlag.

Uzawa, H. 1962. "Walras' Existence Theorem and Brouwer's Fixed Point Theorem" *Economic Studies Quarterly, 13.*

von Neumann, J. 1928. "Zur Theorie der Gesellschaftsspiele" *Mathematische Annalen, 100*, 295-320.

1937. "Uber ein okonomisches Gleichungssystem und eine Verallgemeinerung des Brouwerschen Fixpunktsatzes" *Ergebnisse eines Mathematischen Kolloquiums, 8* (1935-1936), 73-83. [Translation: "A Model of General Economic Equilibrium" *Review of Economic Studies, 13* (1945-1946)].

von Neumann, J. and Morgenstern, O. 1944. *Theory of Games and Economic Behavior.* New York: Wiley.

Wald, A. 1935. "Uber die eindeutige positive Losbarkeit der neuen Produktionsgleichungen" *Ergebnisse eines Mathematischen Kolloquiums, 6*, 12-18. [Translation: "On the Unique Non-Negative Solvability of the New Production Equations (Part 1)" In *Precursors in Mathematical Economics: An Anthology*, edited by Baumol and Goldfield, London School of Economics and Political Science, 1968.]

1936. "Uber die Produktionsgleichungen der okonomischen Wertlehre" *Ergebnisse eines Mathematischen Kolloquiums, 7*, 1-6. [Translation: "On the Production Equations of Economic Value Theory (Part 2)" In *Precursors in Mathematical Economics: An Anthology*, edited by Baumol and Goldfield, London School of Economics and Political Science, 1968.]

Walker, M. 1977. "On the Existence of Maximal Elements" *Journal of Economic Theory, 16*, 470-474.

1979. "A Generalization of the Maximum Theorem" *International Economic Review, 20*, 260-272.

Walras, L. 1874. *Elèments d'èconomie politique pure.* Lausanne: Corbaz.

Willard, S. 1970. *General Topology.* Reading, Mass.: Addison Wesley.

Yoseloff, M. 1974. "Topologic Proofs of Some Combinatorial Theorems" *Journal of Combinatorial Theory, 17*, 95-111.

Index